The Politics of Social
Program Evaluation

The Politics of Social Program Evaluation

David K. Banner
University of New Brunswick

Samuel I. Doctors
University of Pittsburgh

Andrew C. Gordon
Northwestern University

Foreword by
David B. Hertz

Ballinger Publishing Company ● Cambridge, Mass.
A Subsidiary of J.B. Lippincott Company

This book is printed on recycled paper.

International Standard Book Number: 0-88410-009-X

Library of Congress Catalog Card Number: 74-28452

Printed in the United States of America

Library of Congress Cataloging in Publication Data

Banner, David K
  The politics of social program evaluation.
  Bibliography: p.
  1. Opportunity Funding Corporation. 2. Minority business enterprises—United States—Finance. 3. Evaluation research (Social action programs)—United States—Case studies. I. Doctors, Samuel I., joint author. II. Gordon, Andrew C. III. Title.
  HD2346.U5B25   362.5'0973   74-28452
  ISBN 0-88410-009-X

Contents

List of Figures

List of Tables

List of Abbreviations

CAF (Washington-based Foundation) — Cooperative Assistance Fund

CDCs (OEO) — Community Development Corporations

CEP (Federal Manpower Program) — Concentrated Employment Program

DBL (SBA Loan Program) — Displaced Business Loans

EDA (Department of Commerce) — Economic Development Administration

EDD (OEO) — Economic Development Division

EEOC (Federal Agency) — Equal Employment Opportunity Commission

EOL (SBA Loan Program) — Equal Opportunity Loans

FDIC — Federal Deposit Insurance Corporation

HRD (USES Program) — Human Resources Development Program

JOBS (Federal Private Manpower Program) — Job Opportunities in the Business Sector

LBDO (OMBE Program) — Local Business Development Organization

LDC (SBA Program) — Local Development Company

MCAP (Private Sector Program) — Minority Contractors Assistance Program

MDTA — Manpower Development and Training Act

MESBIC (SBA Program) — Minority Enterprise Small Business Investment Company

NAB (Private Manpower Program) — National Alliance of Businessmen

OEO — Office of Economic Opportunity

OFC (OEO Funded Program) — Opportunity Funding Corporation

OFCC	Office of Federal Contract Compliance
OMBE (Dept. of Commerce)	Office of Minority Business Enterprise
OPD (OEO)	Office of Program Development
PPBS	Planning–Programming–Budgeting System
SBA	Small Business Administration
USES	U.S. Employment Service

Preface

Despite the fact that large outlays of federal monies for social action programs were made during the 1960s, many of the social problems toward which these funds were directed showed little remission. In some cases, the problems worsened. Social planners and administrators increasingly are being required to offer some scientific proof about the effectiveness of their particular technique or approach before the Congress will consider re-funding their agency or program. Evaluation research has come to serve this function of legitimization. Unfortunately, because of the nature of the political environment surrounding evaluation research, "objective" research often proves impossible. Evaluation can become a tool for wielding power and, as such, is constantly an active variable in changing power relationships within the political and organizational structure.

This book stems from an investigation into the scope and impact of this phenomenon. A case study is used as a vehicle for illustrating and analyzing major theoretical points. The research focus for this case was a federally funded, experimentation/demonstration program called the Opportunity Funding Corporation (OFC), administered by the Office of Economic Opportunity (OEO). OFC aims to test the ability of a series of financial leverage devices such as interest subsidies, guarantees, and secondary market activities to encourage a flow of capital *into* ghetto areas (instead of the traditional outflow). As with most OEO programs, the evaluation of OFC's effectiveness in achieving its objectives does play a part in refunding and/or increasing funding appropriations.

We wish to thank all the people at the Opportunity Funding Corporation (including the Board of Directors) for their help and candor during the research phase. Many people at the Office of Economic Opportunity also provided invaluable information. Similarly, those connected with OFC's predecessor, *Project X,* were quite helpful in their openness and frankness. We wish to thank Vera Chatz for her help in editing several versions of the manuscript.

Finally, much valuable data and advice received from various academicians, government officials, consultants, and business people rounded out our data requirements and gave the research credibility and tightness. We offer this book not as a definitive statement on the politics of evaluation but as an introductory exploration into a complex phenomenon that will remain an active process to be dealt with in future social programming.

Foreword

Evaluation, as the *Dictionary of Behavioral Science* points out, is the
determination of the relative value of a phenomenon by appraisal or comparison
with a standard. Thus, the evaluation of the efficacy of a drug in treating a
disease is carried out with statistical comparison procedures that carry the
general stamp of scientific methodology. The attempts to develop similar
procedures for proposed remedies for social ailments have been fraught with
difficulties, obstacles, and political barriers. These are described in this book
by Banner, Doctors and Gordon in the context of the early history of the
Opportunity Funding Corporation (OFC), a demonstration activity established
and funded by the Office of Economic Opportunity (OEO) during the first
Nixon Administration.

The analyses that led to the development of OFC were a product of
the ferment and stresses in the minority and low-income communities during
the 1960s. These analyses, summarized and brought to a set of very specific
conclusions by Ted Cross, clearly pointed to the lack of a financial infrastructure
in such communities (e.g., virtually no indigenous banks or other financial
institutions, cash flows that progressed almost entirely to the affluent business
community, almost no asset ownership, provision of services for the low-income
community by institutions outside the community, although largely paid for by
the community's taxes). Cross recommended to Donald Rumsfeld, then Director
of OEO, that some institution be established to develop the mechanics of risk
reduction that would begin to stimulate the growth of savings, asset ownership,
entrepreneurial activity—in other words, a capitalistic rather than colonial
economy. In this general context, OFC was born, with a charter to experiment
in reducing risk, stimulating the flow of capital, and determining what subsidies
would in fact encourage the growth of permanent capital institutions in the
disadvantaged communities of the United States.

As the authors point out, the charter of OFC included a mandate for evaluation of its efforts by OEO, and by itself. The history and difficulties of such evaluation are described and clearly indicate that OFC was unable to "design" any experiments that would meet any reasonable tests of scientific reliability. The basic reason given is that OFC had to undertake its activities (underpinning surety bonds, formulating financing arrangements for entrepreneurial projects with several parties, developing new mechanisms for partially protecting third parties against risk, among others) in open market environments in many communities all over the country. Further, no one could clearly state what a "scientific" experiment to stimulate the flow of capital would be.

It is difficult enough to perform satisfactory clinical trials on a new drug to determine its efficacy. This is the case even when: (1) the disease being attacked is clearly defined, (2) the using population can be divided into test subjects, a control group and placebos can be utilized to remove subjective bias, and (3) statistical standards can be *pre-established* to test for significance. How much more difficult it is—well nigh impossible—in the context of a broad-scale social experiment to do any of these things.

OFC's Board of Governors, at its foundation, agreed that evaluation was indeed important—that it and OFC's management would welcome whatever mechanisms of evaluation were laid on it by OEO, or whatever it felt it could develop within the context of its resources and subjectivity. It felt that evaluation was too critical to shaping the economic systems of the future to wait for a perfect *method*—one adapted to each experimental project—to be developed. Therefore, it took the view that the overall standard against which each of the kinds of projects should be measured would be "success and cost" as compared to the financial and entrepreneurial environment in the affluent community. Thus, the sound *survival* and development of strong management of OFC itself would be a key measure of success of the experiment (as, for example, the *survival* of the CDC movement is a better measure for that OEO program than the individual analysis of CDC projects).

In a very broad sense, the Board of Governors decided that it would evaluate its success, and direct OEO's attention to that evaluation on a benefit-cost basis. (This, of course, is the most popular of the "methods" for evaluation of public policy programs—not necessarily the best, or even appropriate.) The Board, a dedicated group having business, financial, community and public service backgrounds, established a broad set of demonstration criteria: (1) survival with growing strength, (2) sound financial management of a significant balance sheet, (3) development of financing arrangements with major institutions, (4) attracting non-governmental interest and partnerships. If these were met, then it was felt that the individual programs and projects would be part of a fabric demonstrating the potential contribution of risk reduction to the growth of an asset-creating infrastructure. Virtually all the Board's debates, analyses, decisions and relationships with management have had this end in view.

These objectives touch on significant issues in public economic policy. They reach to the core of the evaluation process. Someone has to decide— *a priori*--what kind of data policymakers need, in both an analytical and political sense, to (a) reshape existing programs, (b) initiate new programs, and (c) allocate resources. Further, in order to proceed with these, there is a public need for (a) quality assessment, (b) quality assurance and, finally, (c) perceived achievement. Without the latter three, no evaluation methods will avail against political forces, either for or against programs.

Since the OFC Board accepted and emphasized the objective of infrastructure and institutional change (as opposed to virtually impossible measurement of individual well-being on the part of the numerous individuals involved in the communities affected), it considered the development of OFC as a force in itself as a key variable. And it recognized that time is essential to institutional and structural change. So, an initial objective was survival in a stronger, healthier form over the first 5 years. This has been achieved.

On all counts, OFC is an institution with a significant place in community development. Its programs have grown and changed significantly. Thus, it has become clear that there is simply too much risk for anything other than pure subsidy or very special arrangements in surety bonding programs for marginal contractors—OFC's loss record parallels everyone else's. There are satisfactory fees to be earned in channelling funds into effective community enterprises. Partnerships can be formed with community groups and foundations. New areas such as communications hold promise for financial experimentation. Finally, there is no substitute in experimental design for good management, which will be sought out by others—witness the present arrangement to manage the Cooperative Assistance Fund, and the ties with Minbanc and the National Urban Coalition.

All of this success notwithstanding, it must be recognized that there is a wide technical and political gulf between the need and the desire to evaluate social experimentation on the one side, and the ability to do so on the other. Many proposed schemes assume that either there exist ready methods of assessment and appraisal or that the technology, manpower, and data can be assembled rapidly for effective evaluation. In my opinion, such assumptions are virtually always proved wrong. If OFC's case is to be taken as an example, then the best approach is to establish the institutional context in which qualitative— and to the extent possible, quantitative—effects on the environment can be noted over long periods of time, just as is done in the medical profession for nonspecific health related programs.

This book deals with the difficulties and complications of carrying out and evaluating new social programs. OFC was an entirely new concept—

nothing like it existed in the government, although there were private funds for profit risk takers (e.g., investment bankers)—and understanding what it was and what it might be was clearly difficult. The authors have dealt with this problem with clarity. And their relationships with OFC management have been extremely helpful for which we in OFC are grateful.

As small as the scale is, it would seem that the key question is whether the country is better off because OFC exists. I believe in the context of any form of evaluation of a social experiment as a whole, the answer that comes out of the detailed analysis of the evaluation process by the authors of this book is a clear "yes".

David B. Hertz
Chairman, Board of Governors
Opportunity Funding Corporation

New York
January 31, 1975

Chapter One

Introduction

Beginning in the early 1960s, the United States government began spending billions of dollars in an attempt to eradicate some of the social problems plaguing society. These monies were used in the areas of health, education, and welfare on various programs that aimed to aid disadvantaged Americans in obtaining job training, unemployment compensation, adequate health care, and the like. Some of these programs were directed at specific target groups (e.g., Head Start, Aid to Dependent Children), while others attempted to promote equality of opportunity "for all Americans." In other words, the program was directed at giving disadvantaged Americans the necessary resources to enter the larger mainstream of American economic and social life. To date, the record of these programs is mixed at best. Despite huge outlays of money, many social problems remain unsolved.

Many demands, not the least of which is national defense, are made upon federal dollars. Defense outlays show no discernible downward trend, so it is safe to conclude that future social action programs will have to come from a rather limited federal budget (barring large increases in tax revenue and/or a flagging desire to fight inflation). Thus, for the foreseeable future, a sometimes heated competition will take place between various social welfare agencies and departments for allocation of existing federal resources. Therefore, a need exists for some objective mthod of ascertaining the ability of a given program to achieve its objectives; the use of such a technique would allow development of a rational system of priorities for fund allocation. To gain continued funding, agency administrators would have to begin justifying their programs with solid evaluation research findings.[1]

Social scientists have been growing uneasy about the validity of many programs being developed under the auspices of "applied social science."[2] The federal government's orientation has been toward "action programs" with an unspoken assumption that given our humanitarian moral posture, the programs surely will do what we ask them to do. It is now becoming clear that this is not always the case. To further complicate the issue, evaluation research has been performed poorly—feedback on what does and does not work has been inconsistent.[3] Experiments have been shoddily designed and poorly implemented. Thus, many agency policymakers have abandoned such evaluations and have measured the efficacy of their programs in terms of "gut reactions." An administrator may back his program and attempt to get renewed funding in the absence of any scientific evidence regarding the program's basic efficacy.

Lastly, as we shall see in this book, even the most carefully designed and well-implemented evaluation research is often sabotaged by factors within the program's political* environment.[4] The nature of the roles various actors feel compelled to play with regard to evaluation creates problems that directly affect the quality of the ultimate research effort. Through the vehicle of the empirical case study, this book aims to investigate the politics of evaluation research. The dynamics of social perception in a political environment are focused upon as an analytical tool. These perceptions are analyzed with an eye towards how people will infer certain attributes or intentions from the information they receive.[5]

Our empirical focus is the Opportunity Funding Corporation (OFC), a non-profit, Office of Economic Opportunity (OEO)–funded program designed to test the ability of a variety of financial techniques, such as loan guarantees and interest subsidies, for the purpose of attracting private capital into disadvantaged areas. OFC is an experimentation/demonstration program whose goal is to ascertain which, if any, of a series of risk-reducing financial techniques can be successful in stimulating a flow of capital into ghetto/barrio areas, thereby providing a base for viable minority economic development. The assumption underlying this model is that it is inherently more risky (because of crime, low-income base, high-cost credit, and so forth) to do business in the ghetto than in the larger economy. OFC intends to offset that risk with incentives and guarantees so that private capital can be attracted to disadvantaged areas. OFC is unique because it is designed to test the effects of *indirect* financial techniques for leveraging OFC money many times and infusing it into the depressed community.

The chronology of OFC analysis takes us from the initial formulation of an evaluation philosophy, through the creation of the evaluation design, to the implementation of some of the major programs in the OFC plan. The effects of the following variables upon organizational decision making with regard to evaluation are studied:

*It is important to note that the word *political* is not used in the perjorative sense. Politics, as is well-documented, is a neutral phenomenon; it only acquires a negative connotation when it is used to describe dishonesty, chicanery, graft, and other "political" problems. Political processes (in this research) refer to the interactions of various actors within the bureaucracies as they relate to each other from different positions of power, influence, and authority.

1. The nature of the power and influence processes exercised within OFC that has affected decision making concerning the evaluation of OFC's programs, beginning with the early "Project X" days and progressing through the successful implementation of major programs.
2. The power and influence processes involved in the network of influential clients and agencies impinging on OFC, from the "Project X" days through 1973.

More specifically, our study is an in-depth examination of the relationships (formal and informal) between several levels of actors located within different bureaucracies as they relate to the evaluation issue at OFC. Based upon his/her position within a bureaucracy (as well as other psychological factors), each actor brings a set of predispositions to the evaluation question. Some have mixed allegiances to both strict evaluation and to program implementation. While not mutually exclusive, these two orientations do tend to be somewhat contradictory. Other actors, in different bureaucracies as well as in OFC, have definitive positions either in favor of rigorous, scientific evaluations of OFC's programs or in support of the successful operation of existing programs and the implementation of new ones (both at the expense of a rigorous evaluation of these programs). This study outlines, in chronological order beginning with the pre–OFC "Project X" days in late 1969 through 1973, the patterns and complexities of the various forces that impinge upon relevant decision making (either formal or informal) with regard to the evaluation of OFC programs.

In this book, such questions as these will receive attention:

1. How have federal agencies historically used evaluation results in their policymaking with regard to social action programs?
2. What is the political impact of a negative evaluation study on agency policymakers? What are their probable response options?
3. What are the political processes involved in designing evaluations that have a high probability of yielding positive results (used to support the status quo)? How about those planned to be negative in outcome (used to kill or weaken the program)? In general, how can social science research be used as a political tool by policymakers and/or those influential on agency policy? How can it be used similarly by politicians?
4. What are the covert effects of evaluation results, attitudinal in nature, that are not reflected in overt political maneuvering?
5. How can operational personnel impede or distort the research process?
6. How can agency policymakers directly and indirectly affect the outcome of an evaluation?
7. Is it possible to alter the political environment of social action programs so that more objective evaluations are possible?

SCOPE OF THE BOOK

Although the theoretical portion of our book relies heavily upon existing research and writings on the politics of evaluation (and the evaluation function itself), the main plan was to let the OFC data speak for itself. In other words, the case study relied primarily on personal interviews and selected secondary sources; the data was then analyzed in light of relevant theory on the politics of evaluation. The data was found to substantiate much of the theoretical work on the politics of evaluation; in addition, several new hypotheses were generated.

The politics of evaluation research may be viewed as a phenomenon of major power and influence centers that manipulate "objective" research to their own advantage. The OFC case has several such centers including (1) people associated with the embryonic "Project X;" (2) the OEO evaluation staff; (3) the management of OFC; (4) the OFC Board of Directors; (5) the Economic Development Division (EDD) of OEO; (6) the OEO general counsel; (7) OEO management; and (8) various consultants to OFC. The empirical design aims to obtain valid and reliable information from each of these power and influence centers and to somehow make sense of their judgments and "factual" information.

LIMITATIONS OF THE RESEARCH APPROACH

As of November 1973, not a single rigorously designed evaluation has been generated on an OFC program. Difficulties (to be discussed later) have prevented completion of even the first evaluation by Boone-Young Associates, a black New York City-based consulting firm hired by OEO to evaluate OFC programs. As of December 1973, only an OFC in-house report of findings had been received by OEO. Therefore, since this empirical study covers the first few years of OFC's organizational life, it obviously cannot make a complete judgment regarding the final disposition of evaluation at OFC (since that is yet to come). The bulk of the research concentrates on political processes surrounding the evaluation question from 1969, and the embryonic "Project X" days, through 1973 to the granting, implementation, and completion of the first evaluation contract at OFC.

The lack of an ability to generalize, that is inherent in a case study approach, provides a second limitation. However, the purpose of this research is to test existing hypotheses about the politics of evaluation and to develop new hypotheses based upon the OFC experience; this goal has been accomplished. This study is exploratory in nature since one of its primary goals is the generation of new hypotheses for future research. The politics of evaluation research have recently begun to receive wide theoretical attention, but there have been very few empirical investigations to substantiate that body of theory.[6] Hopefully, this study will mark a beginning in that direction.

Despite the limitations of the case study approach, there is much to be learned from an intensive, critical examination of one agency in its political environment and the ways in which agency personnel and other interested parties deal with the evaluation question. In many ways, the organizations being studied are similar to the myriad federal and quasi-federal agencies in Washington, and their responses to the evaluation question can provide valuable insights into the political conflicts and compromises involved in evaluating social action programs.

There is yet another limitation to the study. Especially with reference to the "Project X" days, the respondents were asked to recall motives, intentions, and feelings that occurred in the fairly distant past. The difficulties with *ex post facto* designs are well-documented and need no elaboration here.[7] Various attributions and components involved in the initial perception of an event may not be accurately reproduced after a period of time. Consequently, over a period of time, there may be a shift in the stability of the attribution or even in the attribution itself.[8]

JUSTIFICATION FOR THE RESEARCH

The methodological approach to evaluation research is fairly well-elaborated in the pioneering work of Campbell and Stanley.[9] What does require further study are the effects of political power and influence processes within specific bureaucratic environments as they affect the program's evaluation. Through an increased understanding of this process, techniques may be designed that substantially reduce the political threat of evaluation to administrators who are involved with implementation of a social action program. Toward this end, Campbell has suggested that the allegiance of program directors or administrators be directed toward the solution of a particular social problem, rather than toward a specific strategy or program for the problem's solution.[10] By using such an "experimental" posture for viewing his/her role, the agency administrator can avoid having ego involvement in the success or failure of a specific program, and is thus free to change strategies either when it becomes obvious that a certain one is not working, or when a pre-determined period of time has elapsed. The mandate becomes one of correcting the problem rather than implementing a specific program to correct the problem. It is beyond the scope of this book to test Campbell's theory, but such an endeavor certainly seems worthy of research attention.

This book hopefully will add to the existing store of knowledge on bureaucratic decision making concerning a specific, controversial agency issue. By interviewing people selectively and as unobtrusively as possible at the various power and influence centers in OFC's "evaluation environment" (those individuals and agencies directly or indirectly influencing OFC's evaluation), we studied their perceptions concerning how they relate to each other and, more specifically, how they relate to the evaluation function. Such open-ended interviewing uncovered the subjects' difficulties in interfacing with each other at different bureaucratic levels; this is the problem of information and influence transfer from one level of one bureaucracy to the same or different level of another bureaucracy.

As cross-pressures built upon the actors involved in the decision-making process regarding evaluation, it became possible to trace the ultimate disposition of these pressures in terms of conflict and/or compromise behavior. By viewing the power and influence processes between the various "power centers," the complete process can be grasped more fully. During the initial design of the OFC model and subsequent to that time, several individuals and organizations have had an impact upon the evaluation question. Through a systematic examination of the ways in which these individuals and organizations relate to each other, one gets a "real-world" orientation toward the way decision making takes place in the organizational setting.

The assumptions/predispositions concerning evaluation that the various actors bring to the decision-making process are critical. For example, the agency administrator and the evaluator(s) naturally will have different sets of priorities and cognitions about the role of evaluation in a social action program. Hopefully our research will clarify those orientations and will identify how they might change if the principals were to interact in a meaningful dialogue. Related to the issue of assumptions and predispositions is the area of political motives. As actors maneuver in the bureaucratic framework for advantage and/or self-aggrandizement, it is interesting to note their apparent goals and the tactics they employ to achieve these goals.

With the aid of this type of study, it may become possible to design new political environments in which offsetting pressures or tradeoffs might be injected artificially into the situation so that an equilibrium situation can be created. Critics of Campbell's "experimental administrator" (who is oriented toward problem solution) rightly point out that it might be difficult to locate administrators who are not defensive and bureaucratically insecure personality types.[11] For precisely that reason, it might be desirable to design other kinds of environments that are supportive of evaluative research.

METHODOLOGY OF DATA COLLECTION

Since OFC is still a relatively new federally financed organization, it is politically vulnerable to criticism. Because of this, a research study of the scope outlined is dysfunctional for OFC in at least two ways: (1) it consumes a substantial amount of time (interviewing, clearing the use of special information, and so forth), which the staff at OFC might feel would be used more advantageously in tackling organizational problems; and (2) the presence of an "outsider" conducting research influences the respondents' perception of OFC itself. Many authors point to the inevitable way in which the researcher, as well as the research process itself, becomes inexorably enmeshed in the dynamics of organizational life.[12] Since many of OFC's clients are blacks and Mexican-Americans, middle-class, white researchers from a university environment might influence the respondent's perception about OFC and its motives.

For each of the above reasons, it seemed advisable at the outset of the research to implement a quasi-unobtrusive design. In such a design, the researcher uses data collected for some other legitimate or credible reason. Since known observers create reactive effects, they should be removed from the research environment in a manner consistent with quality research standards. Experience has shown this approach to be desirable, especially in politically sensitive environments such as the OEO/OFC interface. The only guideline for the use of this method is that any device, employed in a way that will not harm or discredit a subject but still maintains research credibility, is morally acceptable.[13]

A thorough search of the existing records at OEO in the Project X days, coupled with an abortive attempt to view the actual OFC records, indicated a change in research strategy. With a few notable exceptions, the OEO records bore little fruit with regard to positions taken on the evaluation question. Therefore, the use of selected interviews with key people involved in the evaluation question assumed a primary role. The political vulnerability of OFC received prime consideration during those interviews, and, in that sense, the interviews were as unobtrusive as possible.

Therefore, the strategy for the research emphasized the interview technique but left room for available historical documents, such as minutes of meetings, personal correspondence, or agency memoranda, which were used as supplemental sources for the interviews. Selected interviews were conducted with people who had relevant knowledge concerning the evaluation question at OFC. However, preceding each interview, OFC management was appraised of the interviewers' intended actions so that damaging political repercussions could be avoided or minimized.

TECHNIQUES OF DATA USE

The theoretical material presented in Chapter Three, *The Politics of Evaluation Research,* aims to explain, support, and/or amplify the data uncovered by the interviews and by relevant secondary sources. The OFC case study thereby is put to the test of existing theory and research on the politics of evaluation; a major result of the research is the total or partial support or refutation of this body of knowledge. Specific quotations obtained from the interviews are used extensively throughout the analysis. It must be kept in mind that these quotes represent opinions, not necessarily fact, and they are treated as such in the study.

The data are analyzed using two separate yet complementary analytical tools: sociometric analysis and a correlational method of comparing and contrasting respondent data. A sociometric test is a means of obtaining quantitative data on the preferences of group members in associating with other members.[14] However, for the purposes of this research, a subjectively computed sociogram is used. In other words, the respondents are not asked to make specific choices about such matters as whom they like best in the group. Rather, inferences are drawn from the formal interviews with respect to degrees of association and influence. This rough indication will offer an outline of the power and influence processes among various groups and/or actors in the evaluation environment. Then, using the sociogram as an approximate outline of the dynamics of the interpersonal situation, the correlational analysis is utilized to array the essential elements from the interviews within a meaningful analytic framework.

GENERAL PROPOSITIONS

One of the classic provisions of the scientific method is the testing of hypotheses by use of a controlled experimental design. Typically two groups are con-structed—the control group and the experimental group, the latter being as close as possible in content to the former with the exception of the experi-mental variable Y. By observing the differences between the two groups, one can infer causality between the variable Y and the difference between a mea-surement of the experimental group and control group.

This design works quite well in the physical sciences where labora-tory purity and control can be achieved. Its successful use in the social sciences is much more inconsistent. In fact, one observer feels that social scientists are insecure about the rigor of their discipline and that they "borrow the tools" of the physical scientist in order to lend credibility to their research efforts.[15] In any event, the strict application of the scientific method to social research problems is problematic at best.[16] Exogenous variables beyond the control of the experimenter continually confound his results. (The many internal and external threats to validity are discussed in Chapter Two.)

Therefore, the researchers decided that a rigorous, scientifically structured examination of the politics of evaluation using control groups and experimental groups was not feasible. Time and expense constraints would militate against such a massive undertaking. Great problems would have been encountered in trying to gain access to a sufficient number of organizations for adequate sample size—the politics of evaluation sometimes are quite untidy, and many organizations would not care to expose their internal political maneuverings to an outsider. It would be difficult to gain access to similar enough organizations to make up control and experimental groups. Control for the independent variable would be virtually impossible, since many organizational factors appear to be involved in the political process regarding evaluation. Precisely this process complexity led to the ultimate decision to implement the case study approach. What the researcher loses in ability to generalize, is gained in the ability to view the development of a complete process over time.[17]

Because of the foregoing, the authors decided not to test any formal hypotheses in this research. Instead, a series of general propositions or statements was developed about the nature of the politics of evaluation. These statements, divided into those produced by the literature review and those generated by the research itself, are presented below.

Propositions from Literature Search

P. 1. *Historically, evaluation results have not been used in agency policy formulations and/or change.*

P. 2. *Evaluation research is a political tool, depending both upon the perspective and values held by the viewer and upon whether or not the results are (or are anticipated to be) positive or negative toward the program in question.*

The principal protagonists in the politics of evaluation are the administrator (whose job it is to support and implement the program) and the evaluator (whose job it is to be critical of the program).

The evaluators themselves often have political motives—they can "evaluate" a program to effectively kill it, or, conversely, by choosing a design biased toward a successful outcome, they can support a program of their choosing.

The political structure uses evaluation as a political tool. For example, those in power use positive evaluations to authenticate programs that they support; they selectively ignore those findings that are incongruent with their beliefs, and they purposely suppress positive evaluations of programs that they oppose.

P. 3. *Vague or diffuse goal formulation can be a direct result of the politics of evaluation.*

In the presence of vague or diffuse goals, perceptions of different actors at different bureaucratic levels concerning the role of a given social agency color their orientation toward the evaluation function itself.

P. 4. *Evaluation research is most often supported by those policymakers who are assigned to allocate resources among competing programs.*

P. 5.   *Many agency administrators (and/or program designers) assume that their programs work and do not see the need for evaluating a principle that they already know to be true.*

P. 6.   *Because of the politics of evaluation research, it is often naive to assume that proper research leads to policy improvement.*

P. 7.   *Social action programs often are designed with little thought as to how they can be most effective or how the most can be learned from them through quality evaluation research.*

Propositions from Our Research

P. 8.   *Evaluation and operations are mutually exclusive orientations in a practical sense: It would be difficult to find an aggressive, effective administrator who placed a high priority on quality evaluation.*

P. 9.   *Many levels of bureaucracy typically are involved in the politics of evaluation research, each with a somewhat different perspective on the proper role of evaluation.*

P.10.   *Evaluation research can degenerate into intense role playing with no serious commitment to evaluation research by any of the parties involved in the politics of evaluation.*

THE OUTLINE OF THE BOOK

Chapter Two deals with the traditional role (or lack of role) of evaluation research in policymaking. This chapter sets up the development of the predictive model for the case study in Chapter Three, *The Politics of Evaluation Research.* This chapter represents an exhaustive review of the literature on the politics of evaluation. Since such literature is primarily non-empirical in origin, the research is designed to see how well, from a case-study standpoint, the OFC experience matches up with the predictions of leading writers in the field. Chapter Four looks at the way in which OFC fits into the federal context of minority economic development. Three separate streams of development— judicial, legislative, and executive—are analyzed in historical perspective. Next comes the OFC case, which is concerned with developing an accurate chronology of the development of the evaluation function at OFC (Chapter Five). Major actors in the evaluation environment are interviewed, and their statements are liberally supplied to illustrate key points in the politics of evaluation at OFC. Finally, in Chapter Six, the empirical data from the OFC case are arrayed against the predictive model developed in Chapter Two, and recommendations for the depoliticization of the evaluation environment are discussed. The purpose of the Epilogue in Chapter Seven, is to discuss the brief reexamination of conclusions, eighteen months after the empirical investigation was conducted.

NOTES

1. An evaluation is a judgment of worth; it represents an appraisal of a given program's intrinsic value in achieving its stated objectives. See Edward A. Suchman, *Evaluative Research* (New York: Russell Sage Foundation, 1967), p. 2.
2. Ibid., p. 1.
3. Ibid., p. 19.
4. See Carol H. Weiss, "The Politics of Evaluation," unpublished paper prepared for the Midwest Political Science Association Annual Meeting, Chicago, Illinois, April 1972; John W. Evans and Walter Williams, "The Politics of Evaluation," *Annals of the American Journal of Political and Social Science* 385 (September 1969); and John W. Evans, "Evaluating Social Action Programs," in Francis Caro (ed.), *Readings in Evaluation Research* (New York: Russell Sage Foundation, 1971).
5. Harold Kelley, "Attribution Theory in Social Psychology," *Nebraska Symposium on Motivation* (1967), p. 208.
6. See Carol H. Weiss, ed., *Evaluating Action Programs* (Boston: Allyn and Bacon, 1972) for a complete discussion of the need for empirical research into the politics of evaluation.
7. See Donald T. Campbell and Julian C. Stanley, *Experimental and Quasi-Experimental Designs for Research* (Chicago: Rand-McNally, 1963) for a complete review of the various problems associated with field research.
8. Kelley, "Attribution Theory in Social Psychology," p. 205.
9. Campbell and Stanley, *Experimental and Quasi-Experimental Designs for Research.*
10. Donald T. Campbell, "Reforms as Experiments," *Urban Affairs Quarterly* (December 1971), p. 136.
11. Phillip Shaver and Graham Staines, "Problems Facing Campbell's 'Experimental Society,' " *Urban Affairs Quarterly* (December 1971), pp. 173–6.
12. The reactive effects of the research process are well-documented. See Charles Hampden-Turner, *Radical Man* (Cambridge: Schenkman Publishing Co., Inc., 1970) and Eugene J. Webb et al., *Unobtrusive Measures: Non-Reactive Research in the Social Science* (Chicago: Aldine Publishing Co., 1970).
13. Eugene J. Webb, "Unconventionality, Triangulation, and Inference," in Norman K. Denizin (ed.), *Sociological Methods* (Chicago: Aldine Publishing Co., 1970).
14. Paul F. Secord and Carol W. Backman, *Social Psychology* (New York: McGraw-Hill Book Co., 1964), p. 239.
15. See Charles Hampden-Turner, *Radical Man;* especially Chapter I.
16. See Campbell and Stanley, *Experimental and Quasi-Experimental Designs for Research.*

17. See Noralou P. Roos, "Evaluation, Quasi-Experimentation and Public
     Policy: Observations by a Short-Term Bureaucrat," in J.A. Caporaso
     and L.L. Roos, Jr. (eds.), *Quasi-Experiments: Testing Theory and
     Evaluating Policy* (Evanston, Ill.: Northwestern University Press,
     1973), p. 15.

Chapter Two

Evaluation Research and Its Role in Organizational Policymaking

A common complaint of evaluation researchers is that the results of their efforts seldom influence agency policy formulation and/or change. For reasons that we explore later, evaluation results typically are either selectively ignored or rationalized by agency policymakers. Even when evaluation results are used in policymaking, a political motive for their use often transcends the desire for simply improving the performance of a given program.

For these reasons, we do not deal with organizational policymaking in any substantive theoretical or practical sense. Instead, we focus first on a conceptualization of the evaluation research process and then on an examination of some structural reasons that explain why such research does not seem to play a part in a given agency's policy deliberations. The ideal role of evaluation research is examined here, as are the organizational and political constraints that effectively preclude the reaching of such an ideal. This macro-approach to the problems of evaluative research in influencing policy will be followed in Chapter Three by a more detailed exposition of the politics of evaluation.

THE PROCESS OF EVALUATION RESEARCH

Evaluation measures the extent to which a program realizes certain goals. In other words, the evaluation process assigns a value to some objective and then determines the degree of success achieved by a policy action or program in achieving that objective. This, of course, constitutes the problem of "separating out" specific effects attributable to a given policy action from a program's total output. Evaluation research has used the scientific method as its basic analytical tool in determining effects. Since the real world does not have the experimental purity of a controlled laboratory situation, quasi-experimental designs have been used to maximize a given research situation.[1] Because of the difficulties inherent in the field of research environment, there has been an increased use of these quasi-experimental designs as well as a heightened interest in such qualitative studies as systems studies, historical analyses, and case studies.[2]

The evaluation process begins with an identification of the goals to be evaluated.[3] This seems obvious, but it is, in fact, an extremely complex and value-laden undertaking. Initially, there is the issue of overt versus covert goals. If the evaluator measures only the stated or overt goals of a program, he may completely miss benefits that might typically accrue in other areas or because of synergy with existing programs. For this reason, the goal set of a particular program should include both overt program goals and those covert goals that while not stated, are important products of a program's operation.

Our methodologies become relatively ineffectual when faced with the measurement of many simultaneous goals. Yet a narrow unigoal orientation may mask many good points at the expense of a few bad ones. The very difficult problems of selecting goals, formulating operational definitions of these goals, and developing quantitative indices against which the program can be rated sometimes overwhelm the would-be field researcher.

As a first step, there must be a complete analysis of the problems with which the activity must cope. Given this scenario, a description and standardization of these activities should follow. Agency preferences for certain goals would ideally rank them in a priority system so that cirteria for measuring those goals can be developed. Next in the process comes the measurement of the degree of change that takes place. In this step, the change not only has to be measured, but it also must be linked causally with some independent variable. In other words, the experimenter must insure, as far as possible, that the change was not produced by some unlikely sequence of events or by some other extraneous variable not controlled by the design. This is the critical step of determining causality: Was the observed change due to the activity or to some other cause(s)? Finally, the process ends with some indication of the durability of the effects. This also is a critical determination. The Head Start evaluation study by Westinghouse concluded that the children might have experienced attitudinal and cognitive growth from the program, but the effects were so transitory as to be useless.[4]

A slightly different perspective exists for viewing the process of evaluation.[5] First comes *value formation.* Our values determine what we regard as problems (as well as what are *not* problems) and determine how best to solve them. This internally consistent set of values leads directly to *goal setting,* the statement of objectives reflecting the value posture. Next comes the *specification of goal-measuring criteria* by which the program's success or failure in achieving its goals can be assessed. *Identification of the goal activity* or program planning comes next. In this step, the *actual programs are delineated* carefully. These programs reflect a judgment of those activities that would most probably lead to goal attainment with the smallest possible expenditures of time and money expended (if these are important constraints). *Program implementation* is the next step, followed by *program evaluation* or the process of assessing the degree of goal attainment achieved by the program. Program evaluation ideally has a feedback effect in which the initial value structure that started the process is either altered or reinforced by the results of the evaluation. This is a circular process or a closed system.[6] From this scenario, we can conclude that evaluation is a normative, subjective process, since evaluation is based on program implementation, which is based on objectives, which are, in turn, based upon value assumptions.[7]

A final perspective is perhaps the most valuable of the three, since it focuses specifically on the relationship of the evaluator, the program objectives, and the policymaker. A simple, useful model of evaluation is used. This evaluation research model systematically relates program inputs to program outcomes, or, more specifically, program impacts.[8] The model assumes that the policymaker wishes to achieve an objective, such as "more efficient delivery of health care."[9] Of course, there may be several objectives, such as changing the delivery of health care, improving efficiency, improving quality, and improving access. A second part of the evaluation model is a consideration of alternative means for achieving these objectives. As a minimum, the alternatives examined may constitute only implementation of Program X as opposed to lack of implementation. The implementation of several alternative programs could also be examined. The third element of the model is impact analysis that focuses on the program or combination of programs delivering most of the objective(s). The final part of the model is implementation of research results. This assumes that the policymaker or administrator will be influenced by evaluation research. The research should help decide which programs to fund or to curtail, which law(s) to enact, and which to veto.

Assumptions of Evaluation Research
Two questions should be asked about program success:

1. Is it working? This is the test of *validity*.
2. Is it good? This is the test of *value*.

Validity relates to the program's performance as compared with the program objectives, while value refers to a system of beliefs concerning what is "good" or what represents "success." Practically speaking, evaluative research can only address itself to the first question. Someone, or some group, which is charged with determining the value of "good" societal outcomes must deal with the second question.

To fully serve its function, evaluation research must ask the following questions:[10]

1. *What is the nature of the content of the objective?* Are we interested in producing exposure, awareness, interest or action?
2. *Who is the target of the program?* Do you want to change individuals, groups, or whole communities? Do you want to aim directly at the target or get at it indirectly?
3. *When is the desired change to take place?* Should the program have immediate effect? Intermediate? Long-term? What about side effects?
4. *Are the objectives unitary or multiple?* Do you aim for a single change or a series of changes?
5. *What is the desired magnitude of the changes?* Should they be widespread or concentrated? What percentage of effectiveness is to be considered "success"?
6. *How is the objective to be obtained?* What means are necessary to put the program into effect? Will you depend upon voluntary cooperation or will you need legal sanction? Will personal or impersonal, formal or informal, appeals be made?

To summarize, evaluation research asks about the *kinds* of change desired, the *means* by which the change is to be brought about, and the *signs* by which the change can be recognized.[11] Evaluation should raise not only the question—*Did the program succeed?*—but it should also ask—*Why did a given strategy fail or succeed?* This requires an analysis of:

1. The dimensions of the program;
2. The differential impact of the program on the population(s) exposed to it;
3. The milieu in which the program took place;
4. The multi-dimensional effects of the program in terms of the short- and long-term effects, attitudinal, and/or behavioral changes, and so forth.

With reference to the aforementioned Westinghouse *Head Start* study, the short-term effects of the program appear good, but they do not appear to be durable. One must ultimately ask how valuable this type of result is for social amelioration.

Types of Evaluation Research

Several strategies have been developed for conducting evaluation research at the federal agency level. Of special interest are the OEO model, developed at the Office of Economic Opportunity, and the model developed by Joseph Wholey at the Urban Institute.

The OEO model is a threefold scheme into which all evaluations may be categorized.[12] Type I is the assessment of the program's overall impact and effectiveness, with emphasis on determining the extent to which programs are successful in achieving their basic objectives. Type II evaluation is the study of the relative effectiveness of different program strategies and variables, with the emphasis on determining which alternative techniques are most productive in carrying out a program design. Type III is the evaluation of individual projects through site visits and other monitoring activities, with the focus on assessing managerial and operational efficiency.

Type I evaluations are designed to be done by the Office of Research, Plans, Programs and Evaluation (RPP&E), an independent entity that functions as an extension of the Director's Office. This is done because if the responsibility for Type I evaluations were left to the program administrator, they would not get done.[13] The program offices themselves are responsible for conducting Type II and Type III evaluations.

The philosophy underlying the selective delegation of the evaluation function merits comment. As noted, Type I evaluations are crucial to policy decisions concerning continuance or curtailment of a given program. Hence, the program administrator's lack of objectivity concerning its impact would likely be substantial. However, much very useful and helpful evaluation data can be collected by the agency itself in Types II and III. Drastic dissonance between the results of the Type I and the Types II/III should indicate the need for further evaluation, preferably by an outside consultant.

Three types of evaluation parallel the three major organization levels and the different types of decisions required at each level.[14] At the top level, the question (Type I) is *What programs?* At the level of the program director, the question (Type II) is *What techniques?* At the regional or local level, the question (Type III) is *What projects?*

The Wholey model, from the Urban Institute, is similar in style of the OEO model.[15] This four-part model contains program impact evaluation, program strategy evaluation, project evaluation, project rating. *Project impact evaluation* is the assessment of a national program's overall effectiveness in meeting its objectives, or the assessment of the relative effectiveness of two or more programs in meeting common goals (Type I). This type of evaluation aims to assist policymakers in reaching decisions on program funding levels or on possible redirection of a program. *Program strategy evaluation* is the assessment of the relative effectiveness of different techniques used in a national program (Type II). This evaluation type aims to inform program managers of the relative effectiveness of the different strategies or methods used by projects in the national program. *Project evaluation* (Type III) is the assessment of the effectiveness of an individual project in achieving its stated objectives. *Project rating* (an extension of Type III) is the assessment of the relative effectiveness of various local projects in achieving program objectives. This type of evaluation usually aims to provide program managers with information on the relative success of local projects operating within a national program.

EVALUATION RESEARCH IN
AGENCY POLICYMAKING

Ideally, an intrinsic relationship exists between evaluation and program planning and development.[16] Evaluation research provides the basic information for designing and redesigning action programs. Thus, evaluation research endeavors to increase our understanding of the applied or administrative processes through a feedback loop, mistakes in policy being modified through clues yielded by the evaluation research. This section deals mainly with the *ideal* relationship between evaluation and policymaking. This book attempts to clarify such differences as may exist between this ideal and the "real-world" situation (hopefully pinpointing reasons for the difference in the process).

There are several ideal uses for the results of an evaluative study.[17] The first and primary concern is to discover whether or how well the objectives of the program are being fulfilled. Implicit in this goal is the determination of specific reasons for failure or success. In this way, the evaluator is able to uncover the principal variables underlying a successful (or unsuccessful) program. The skillful evaluator can direct the course of the experiments with techniques for increasing the program's effectiveness and thus lay the basis for further research on the reasons for the relative success of alternative techniques. The evaluative research results also can help redefine the means to be used in reaching the program's objectives and even in redesigning sub-goals in light of research findings.

Evaluation research is the art of the possible;[18] it is designed to improve decisions by doing the best that can be done in a timely and relevant way. Because of its value in agency policymaking, evaluation should be a central part of the management process and should be given a superordinate position within government agencies. Those involved in evaluation should be provided adequate funding, professional staff, and other necessary resources.[19]

Some Problems with the Ideal
Evaluation-Policy Model
As stated previously, the evaluation research model focuses upon systematically relating program inputs to program outcomes, or, more specifically, program impacts. Two important requirements of this model are that (1) the research be valid and that (2) it be useful to policymakers or administrators.[20] Let us examine the implications of each of these requirements.

Researchers consider validity to be of prime importance. Usefulness is equally important to the policymaker. Usefulness is related to validity, but it must encompass such intangibles as (1) What type of information is the policymaker willing to use and (2) what channels are available for providing the information to the policymaker in a timely fashion? Obviously, information that is not used because it is unacceptable or outdated is of little value in upgrading program effectiveness.

Researchers feel that if the evaluation is not valid, it will be worse than useless to a policymaker—it actually may lead him astray. An equally strong argument can be made about the need for usefulness: If evaluation efforts are ignored by the decision maker, their validity is somewhat beside the point.

Unfortunately, validity and usefulness are probably somewhat incompatible objectives. The time and resources necessary to obtain valid results acceptable to researchers often make such efforts dated and useless to policymakers. Similarly, policymakers (by design or default) frequently confuse public relations with evaluation research. In their quest for meeting immediate policy needs, they are content with superficial evaluations that beg questions of validity. Therefore, basic differences relating to the needs of these two groups cause structural problems that are exceedingly difficult to resolve (if, indeed, they can be resolved). Arriving at some compromise between these conflicting requirements seems to be the optimal solution.

There are other difficulties. In most federal evaluation activities, *ad hoc* evaluations are commissioned with little possibility for making comparisons between programs.[21] Evaluation researchers are somewhat ambiguous in their treatment of program alternatives. Much of the research has focused upon a single program and has addressed the question "What, if any, effect has the program had?" The failure of such research to affect policymaking may be explained by the fact that policymaking is typically built around the consideration of alternatives.[22] The policymaker might be helped if he knew that a given policy were not producing the anticipated results. It would be extremely useful to provide the policymaker with information enabling him to compare and contrast alternative policies that are addressed to the same objectives. The time, effort and dollar costs of evaluating multiple alternatives far exceed those for single-goal evaluations, so they run afoul of the policymaker's inherent need for timely, useful information. To alleviate this problem, some experts have recommended that evaluation funds be pooled.[23] They propose the elimination of the single-project evaluation in favor of large evaluation studies that use the same methodology to compare findings in various locations.

Since there is a real danger of evaluation saturation, the importance of adapting evaluation research to the needs and preferences of policymakers cannot be overstressed. Agencies that fund much of the evaluation research in the health field are (or should be) becoming skeptical about the payoff from such research. While the importance of developing a valid evaluation research methodology cannot be denied, the methodology must be related to the policy and political realities of the situation. Without this concern, evaluation researchers may continue to discover that huge amounts of research may yield an extremely low payoff in terms of actual effects on operations. An example of such a necessary evaluator compromise is the question of the "most different systems" research design.[24] Policymakers often feel that experimentation and local initiative represent the "American way." It is thought that local institutions will and probably should resist a federal agency's efforts to specify the administration of experimental programs. According to this philosophy, policymakers prefer to select very dissimilar sites in which to test a program; some may include whole states, while others may cover a county or city. This "most different systems" design can establish the external validity and generalizability of results, but there may be major questions as to the equivalence of both independent and dependent variables across widely different systems. Under such circumstances, a "different systems design" may make it more difficult to ascertain whether or not the observed impact of an experimental program is spurious. But, given the preferences of policymakers, it may behoove the evaluation researcher to reassess and further develop the "most different systems" design.

Even if evaluation efforts can be designed to feed into the appropriate policy level, organization research indicates that a learning cycle must be completed.[25] The use of the scientific method and the data it generates is foreign to most agency administrators who have had formal academic training in areas other than the sciences. In the absence of such data, policymakers may rely on other types of indicators, or they just may not do all that is possible in using the data.

The point is, for most agency administrators, evaluation data does not fill an existing need. They have managed without such data for a long time by making "gut" decisions, and they must learn to make effective use of scientific evaluations in their policy deliberations. The reverse also seems true: Agencies with experience in data analysis may come to view evaluation as an integral part of decisionmaking. Once policymakers are accustomed to using systematic data, they begin to require such data before they enter into a major policy formulation and/or change effort. They rely upon data for pinpointing problems, for developing a shared perspective on these problems, for using it as a resource while seeking changes in the system and, last but not least, for taking the blame as an impersonal scapegoat in the event of policy failure. This danger is real; data can be "oversubscribed" by responsibility-shy policymakers.

There is a final, extremely important reason for administrators to ignore evaluation results in their policy deliberations. Quite simply, administrators will ignore anything that puts them in a bad light, either by criticizing existing efforts or by pointing to new, possibly more fruitful areas of endeavor that are outside the administrator's competence or interest. This is the subject of the next chapter, the politics of evaluation research.

THE FUTURE OF EVALUATION RESEARCH IN THE SOCIAL AGENCY SETTING

Ultimately, evaluation is the wave of the future. Evaluation reports are becoming frontpage news.[26] Policy decisions are becoming increasingly dependent on the outcome of research. The Westinghouse–Ohio University evaluation of

Head Start made waves at the White House. While evaluators often still bemoan the fact that policymakers ignore the results of their research, they are more and more, either directly or indirectly, being given an active role in decision making. Increasingly, legislation and administrative regulations require evaluation of social programs, large sums of public monies are expended, and results are publicized and considered in decision-making councils.[27] People increasingly will demand an end to social problems, and insecure federal bureaucrats will be forced either to have their programs evaluated (even to their despair) or to lose their jobs.[28]

Many other reasons exist for the growing interest in evaluation. First of all, limited national budget resources are allocated among competing programs, and national defense interests threaten to keep defense spending very high. Therefore, there are only limited funds with which to ameliorate the many social problems. Increasingly, objective research results will serve as the measuring stick to determine who gets what in the allocation process.

Participatory government also seems to be on the rise as a social phenomenon. Citizens are becoming increasingly disenchanted with the failures of bureaucratic liberalism and its paternalistic solutions, and they want answers that work. Americans will continue to demand that something be done about their pressing social problems.

Another factor that will increase the need for evaluation is the significant change in the nature of social problems.[29] Our social problems now affect all members of a community rather than merely an isolated few—Marshall McLuhan's "global village" concept.[30] Institutions bear a major responsibility for our collective social misery, and institutional reform seems to some a better technique for solving these problems than do individual behavioral/attitude changes.[31]

Furthermore, major changes in the structure and function of social agencies argue for the use of evaluation [32] due to a trend toward broader community involvement in programs (alluded to earlier) and a concomitant broader scope in the programs themselves. The need to strengthen programs is increasing together with the concomitant increase in their breadth and complexity. As those in public service acquire both advanced training and professional pride in their fields of specialization, the demand for evaluation and objective "proof" of the validity of their techniques will increase.

In addition, major increases have taken place in the public's sophistication and level of social awareness.[33] Large portions of the public appear to be less and less tolerant of inequities and social injustice. In this same vein, they are more aware of the repressive nature of some of their institutions and will no longer proceed on faith or on the "word" of a government official. Coupled with this increased skepticism about the credibility of official sources and their programs is a heightened public expectation of bigger and better public services. Such services are increasingly being viewed as public rights rather than as individual services or privileges. These current trends in public service and community action tend to reinforce each other and to indirectly produce an ever increasing demand for evaluation research.

However, the demand for evaluation research and the effective use of evaluation research in agency decision making are two vastly different considerations. In fact, the above process may prove quite deceptive. The issue of quantity versus quality becomes paramount with regard to evaluation research. The forces described above are tending to *coerce* agency planners to do evaluations of their programs. Nowhere is the *commitment* of these officials guaranteed. This is a critical variable as we shall see in the next chapter, the *Politics of Evaluation*. Doing an evaluation to satisfy a requirement is not the same as doing an evaluation to improve decision making about a given program. For example, in the OFC study to be taken up later:

> The only time evaluation gets used for decision making is the Project Review Board. There, the analyst, general counsel, and a representative of Planning, Research and Evaluation address the *question of refunding programs.* [34]

If this is the only input of evaluation into the social agency hierarchy, it is difficult to see how it will materially affect agency policy toward more effective implementation of social programs.

The whole evaluation environment easily can be reduced to a game-like atmosphere with everyone going through the motions of "objective evaluation research," but with no commitment to rigorous research design or implementation on the part of the parties to the evaluation. It is with this warning that we introduce the topic that most directly interferes with the completion of an objective evaluation research in a social action program—*the politics of evaluation.*

NOTES

1. See Donald T. Campbell and Julian C. Stanley, *Experimental and Quasi-Experimental Designs for Research* (Chicago: Rand-McNally, 1963) for a complete review of quasi-experimental designs and their application.
2. Robert S. Weiss and Martin Rein, "The Evaluation of Broad-Aim Programs: Difficulties in Experimental Design and an Alternative," in C.H. Weiss (ed.), *Evaluating Action Programs* (Boston: Allyn and Bacon, 1972), p. 248.
3. For a complete description of the process, see G.M. Carstairs, "Problems of Evaluative Research," in J. Williams and C. Ozarin (eds.), *Community Mental Health* (San Francisco: Jossey-Bass, 1968), p. 21.

4. See John W. Evans and Walter Williams, "The Politics of Evaluation: The Case of Head Start," *Annals of the American Journal for Political and Social Science* (September 1969), for a fine analysis of this politically volatile program.

5. Edward A. Suchman, *Evaluative Research* (New York: Russell Sage Foundation, 1968), p. 45.

6. Ibid., p. 34.

7. Ibid., p. 45.

8. Noralou Roos, "Evaluation, Quasi-Experimentation and Public Policy: Observations by a Short-Term Bureaucrat," in J.A. Camporaso and L.L. Roos, Jr. (eds.), *Quasi-Experiments: Testing Theory and Evaluating Policy* (Evanston, Ill.: Northwestern University Press, 1973), p. 3.

9. Ibid.

10. Suchman, *Evaluative Research*, p. 39.

11. Reginald K. Carter, "Client's Resistance to Negative Findings and the Latent Conservative Function of Evaluation Studies," *The American Sociologist* (May 1971), p. 118.

12. John W. Evans, "Evaluating Social Action Programs," *Social Science Qtr.,* Vol. 50, (Dec. 1969), p. 572.

13. Ibid.

14. Ibid., p. 573.

15. Joseph S. Wholey et al., *Federal Evaluation Policy* (Washington, D.C.: The Urban Institute, 1970), pp. 24–25.

16. Suchman, *Evaluative Research*, p. 30.

17. Stanley K. Bigman, "Evaluating the Effectiveness of Religious Programs," *Review of Religious Research* (1961), p. 99.

18. Evans, "Evaluating Social Action Programs," p. 578.

19. Ibid., pp. 578–84.

20. Roos, "Evaluation, Quasi-Experimentation and Public Policy".

21. Wholey, *Federal Evaluation Policy*.

22. Roos, "Evaluation, Quasi-Experimentation and Public Policy," p. 10.

23. Wholey, *Federal Evaluation Policy*.

24. Roos, "Evaluation, Quasi-Experimentation and Public Policy," p. 17.

25. Ibid., p. 21.

26. Carol H. Weiss, "The Politicization of Evaluation Research," in C.H. Weiss (ed.), *Evaluating Action Programs* (Boston: Allyn and Bacon, 1972), p. 327.

27. Ibid., p. 328.

28. Evans, "Evaluating Social Action Programs."

29. Suchman, *Evaluative Research*, p. 3.

30. See Marshall McLuhan, *The Gutenberg Galaxy* (Toronto: University of Toronto Press, 1962) or McLuhan and Quentin Fiore, *The Medium is the Message* (New York: Bantam Books, 1967) for a complete articulation of the "global village" concept.

31. Suchman, *Evaluative Research.*
32. Ibid.
33. Ibid., p. 4.
34. Interview with Dick Cheney, Cost of Living Council, Washington, D.C.,
        May 25, 1972.

Chapter Three

The Politics of Evaluation Research

Evaluation has explicit political overtones. It is designed to yield conclusions about the worth of a given social action program, and in so doing, it is intended to effect the allocation of resources. The purpose of this chapter is to examine the major literature in the politics of evaluation with an eye towards building a model of the process involved. This "model" explores the dimension of political interaction in the evaluation of social action programs.

EVALUATION AND THE SOCIAL AGENCY
DECISION-MAKING PROCESS

In the not-so-distant past, innovative social action programming and its evaluation were small-scale operations. The impact of evaluation might have gone no further than to recommend continued study of a particular deviant behavior, for example, or to discourage a certain form of counseling. The effects tended to be limited, since programs and their evaluations were bounded by limited program size.

The Role of the Planning-Programming-Budgeting
System (PPBS)

Two factors coalesced to change this situation. First, with President Lyndon Johnson's War on Poverty in the early 1960s, "there was the implicit premise . . . that effective programs could be launched full-scale, and could yield significant improvements in the lives of the poor."[1] Speeches rang with hope; basic changes seemed well within our grasp. This period represented a high point in Americans' faith in the nation's ability to bring about significant social change via massive governmental programs implemented on a national scale.

The second factor was the introduction of the Planning-Programming-Budgeting System (PPBS). Designed in the early 1960s by then Defense Secretary Robert MacNamara with the aid of a group of Defense Department "whiz kids," the concept was based on the premise that the decision-making process could be rationalized effectively—that is, rigorous analysis could produce an informational flow that would be instrumental in improving the basis for decision making in organizations. In 1965, President Johnson (through Bureau of the Budget Bulletin #66-3) established this system within all governmental departments and agencies. The departments and agencies were instructed to develop an adequate central staff for analysis, planning, and programming, with the head of the central analytical staff directly responsible to the head of the agency or his deputy. The notion of evaluating the effectiveness of both ongoing programs and new program concepts is central to the PPBS approach.

But the most fundamental political issues arise when evaluation is brought into the agency policymaking process. The results can be viewed as a threat by those who are in established decision-making positions. Unfavorable evaluation results may restrict a program's funds or may force major changes in the program's direction. Thus, a conflict inevitably emerges between those who operate programs (and believe in them) and those who analyze them (whose job it is to be skeptical of them).

As noted in Chapter Two, evaluation research relates program inputs to program outcomes. The policymaker or administrator is the intended consumer of such research, and the research must satisfy the two requirements of validity and usefulness to the administrator. Unfortunately, validity and usefulness probably are not compatible objectives.[2] So much time and resources must be invested in order to obtain results that are acceptable to researchers that such efforts are of marginal value to policymakers. Conversely, administrators (either through design or insufficient knowledge) often confuse public relations with good evaluation research. In their quest to meet operating and policy needs, administrators sometimes are content with superficial evaluations that have questionable validity. The introduction of PPBS into the social action arena brought into focus some basic problems associated with the implementation of action programs and the measurement of their results.

The situation concerning social action programming and its evaluation thus changed markedly during the Johnson years (1963–1968). Programs became national in scope, funded with millions (sometimes billions) of federal dollars. Evaluation also became large scale and was no longer limited to "pilot" or "demonstration" programs. With studies of this scope and the concomitant expense, it is not unexpected that some fanfare attend their completion. The evaluator, unaccustomed to the political spotlight (since, in the past, his work was merely ignored), found old difficulties exacerbated and new problems unfolding.

Overview of the Political Environment for Evaluation
We should not assume from the foregoing that the political environ-

ment for evaluation contains only two protagonists, the evaluator and the administrator. There are others as well. Evaluation, when used as a political tool, is just one way of wielding power and, as such, is an active variable in changing power relationships within both the political and organizational structures. Actually, the evaluation environment can be defined as being composed of three primary influence centers, each with its own political motives: (1) the evaluator, (2) the administrator, and (3) the political structure.

Evaluation can be a tool for the existing political structure. For example, the Bureau of the Budget does many evaluations of social action programs. However, we can assume that those evaluations have a tendency to be biased in favor of the existing administration's ideology (since the Administration appoints the Director of the Bureau). The political structure can be greatly affected by negative evaluations. They can be used to eliminate programs and/or they can be used to preserve the status quo.

The evaluators' motives also are important to the politics of evaluation. Politics is a competitive business, and it is possible for evaluators to "get a name" by discrediting the program of a powerful political figure. We know that the questions we ask (and those we do not ask) and the experiments we design can be heavily biased toward "discovering" the answer we seek.[3] This potential makes the evaluator an active political figure in the evaluation environment. In fact, in terms of political advantage, it can be argued that it is much safer to make a name for oneself as an "objective evaluator" rather than as an administrator who is vulnerable to real or perceived failure.

A final area in the political environment for evaluation is the selection of program goals and the criteria for measuring them. The development of criteria for "success" is a tricky political issue. Program goals are politically established through compromise; politicians are not merely captives of the bureaucracy.[4] Evaluations, while often absent in agency policymaking, sometimes are selectively used to resolve conflicts over determining appropriate values, goals, and criteria for measuring those goals in a given program.

THE IMPACT OF NEGATIVE
EVALUATION FINDINGS

"Trapped administrators" are those whose political predicament will not allow the risk of failure.[5] These administrators are committed to the efficacy of a specific reform or program by the political structures. They are committed to a particular *technique* for solving a social problem. Campbell notes, "It is one of the most characteristic aspects of the present situation that specific reforms are advocated as though they were certain to be successful."[6] These people must be program advocates as well as program administrators. Because their jobs, as well as their careers, hang in the balance, these "trapped administrators" can scarcely be passive observers to evaluation. They may try to prevent evaluation from occurring. If this fails, they may sabotage the evaluation so that, at worst, the findings are inconclusive, or, at best, they show the program to be operating beautifully. To do this, administrators may hire evaluators who will produce the "right" results.

To counteract this problem, Campbell recommends that "experimental administrators" replace "trapped administrators." These experimental administrators would be committed to the idea of solving the problem, rather than to any specific solution. Because of their lack of ego-involvement in any specific problem solution, they would be free to try one solution and then scrap it in favor of another if the first solution proved unsuccessful. The emphasis would be on the importance of the problem and its ultimate solution, rather than on the certainty of a particular answer.

The "latent conservative function" of evaluation describes the clients' inherent resistance to negative research findings.[7] This latent function is said to conform to these rules:

1. The greater the perceived threat to the manager's or client's positive self-concept, the greater will be the resistance to negative findings.
2. The greater the distance between the client's or manager's concept of the social reality being studied and the actual research findings, the greater will be the resistance to the results.
3. The greater the importance or salience to the client or manager of the function being evaluated, the greater the perceived threat to his/her positive self-concept and the greater the resistance to negative findings.

Evaluations often perform a formal legitimization function. If a manager can be sure of a positive finding from the evaluation of the program(s), then the "scientific legitimization" will most assuredly be sought. If evaluations serve this function, they reinforce the status quo and necessarily retard the possibility of change within the organization.

There is little evidence to suggest that evaluation findings have been a major catalyst for change in program design for any social action agency. One reason for this lies in the capacity of a bureaucracy operating within a political structure to manage both the course of the program and the will of its participants. Once the staff employees perceive the strength of management's commitment to a given program, they quickly do what they think they should to avoid incurring the wrath of the "leader." Once subordinates (or researchers, for that matter) within an organization become aware of the rigidity of top management, they may choose to distort and/or selectively report only the information that supports the status quo. In other words, once this latent function becomes obvious to respondents, the quality of evaluation data deteriorates markedly.[8] The respondents will say what they think they should be saying, rather than what they know to be fact. Once this happens, evaluation studies become a ritualistic ceremony to reinforce the false image that top management actively supports "scientific evaluations."

However, it is naive to assume that top management is by definition rigid and that the change impetus comes from the middle levels. According to Professor Frank Cassell, Northwestern University, administrators often are not in favor of the status quo; they are merely in favor of *their brand of change.* He argues that the real rigidity comes from the middle levels of an organization. In this regard, it is important to distinguish between the "political administrator" and the "career administrator" in terms of their reactions to the evaluation issue. The political administrator is temporary and knows it; his/her job may be due to the spoils system. The career administrator, on the other hand, rises through the bureaucratic structure, outlives political administrations and has to live with the results of his work. Both types of administrators would fear negative evaluations, but it would seem logical that the career administrator would be less likely to favor bias and/or fail to report the results of evaluations.

Evaluation findings in the Westinghouse–Ohio University report on Head Start raise two important political questions: (1) What happens when a politically popular program meets with unfavorable evaluation and (2) since a field evaluation is by definition less rigorous than its laboratory counterpart, how is the debate over the accuracy of the findings ultimately resolved, if at all?

The controversy surrounding the Westinghouse–Ohio University study reflects a clash over two sets of ideas—that is, the classic confrontation between the implementers (administration) and the evaluators.[9] The Westinghouse–Ohio University evaluation showed that Head Start children, who when studied were in the first, second, and third grades, *differed little* over time on a series of academic achievement and attitudinal measures from children who had not attended Head Start as three- and four-year olds. From these results it was strongly argued that the social action program did not achieve its objectives.

Evans and Williams feel that Head Start failed, and that it failed because of a series of problems:

1. "We had neither the experience nor the realization of the difficulties involved in developing effective techniques for social action programs . . . we could do the grandiose outlines but had a lot of trouble developing the nitty-gritty detail of technique and organization."
2. Because the program achieved almost instantaneous popularity with the nation, it ballooned from the original concept of an experimental program, with a small number of children involved, into a $100 million project almost overnight.
3. As a result, Head Start—as a large-scale operation—was poorly conceived; however, in the eyes of the public and the program administrators, the popularity of the program was equated with program success.

Evans and Williams comment disparagingly on program level evaluations undertaken in the formative stages of Head Start. These evaluations revealed an improvement in Head Start children. But Evans and Williams argue against the significance inputed to these results, saying that there were test–retest artifacts present, and it was felt the Head Start children had a tendency to help their non-Head Start classmates.[10] Then, in 1967, OEO established a central evaluation division (Office of Research, Plans, Programs, and Evaluation, or RPP&E) to determine the program's overall impact. This met with great resistance at the program level because the agency administrators resented an outside, uninvolved evaluation of their program.

But a lengthy series of criticisms has been directed toward the Westinghouse–Ohio University study as well, including the following:

1. An *ex post facto* design, which is much weaker than a longitudinal study, but can be done more quickly, was used. A control group was generated by matching former HS children with other non-HS children, thereby creating a superior non-HS group and biasing the results.
2. The test instruments were primitive. (Evans and Williams say that is the state of the art.)
3. The effects of Head Start were probably very good but were temporary because when the children returned to their repressive ghetto environment, the gains were wiped out (the children were tested after they left Head Start).
4. Control children were indirectly helped by HS children. HS children inspired their peers with greater motivation, and their mere presence in a class caused the teacher to do a better job and upgrade the quality of teaching.
5. The evaluation was too narrow—it failed to take into consideration such Head Start goals as health, nutrition, and community involvement.
6. The study did not recognize that a variation exists among Head Start programs across the country due to different program styles and characteristics. By publishing a gross condemnation of the total program, the "good" programs are obscured and, more importantly, the variables that make up the difference between successful and unsuccessful programs are also obscured.
7. The sample was too small. It would take massive differences between HS and non-HS children to reach a satisfactory level of statistical significance.
8. The sample was not representative—many of the original randomly selected centers were eliminated from the sample for a variety of administrative
9. Campbell and Erlebacher argue that "regression artifacts" can make a good program look bad when an adjusted covariance analysis is applied to the data [11] Pre-existing differences between experimental and control subjects cannot be separated from treatment effects in this manner, and resulting under adjustments mimic treatment. Campbell and Erlebacher believe that the control subjects were therefore pre-destined to achieve better than the

Head Start pupils. More generally systematic underadjustments in compensatory programs can generate artifacts which appear as null or even harmful effects.

In contrast, Evans and Williams argued that the Westinghouse–Ohio University study—even with its admitted methodological weaknesses—is sound. While maintaining that field research cannot achieve laboratory purity, they argue that the criticisms leveled at this work could be made of any social science research. The mere fact that they were argued with with such fervor indicates the popularity of the program and the political sensitivity of evaluation research with negative findings. The results, they argue, are valid, and should be heeded, but people are unwilling to admit that such a popular program does not work the way it is supposed to work. Their point is that while the attacks on the Westinghouse study were methodological in form, they were essentially ideological in concern.[12] . Since the program symbolized the "War on Poverty" it is understandable that many should rush to the defense of a humane (but unsuccessful) attempt at amelorioration.

The important point in all this for our purposes, and one on which all commentators agree, is the political consequences of program evaluation. Evaluation itself is a political act, from the initial decision that an evaluation should be conducted, through all steps to the ultimate conclusion and dissemination of the evaluation results. The Head Start study is an important instance, not because it is different in its essential character from less well known evaluations, but because the tenacious concern of all parties allowed the full revelation of a variety of issues often otherwise obscured.

In this case politicians, researchers and bureaucrats alike opposed the Westinghouse Ohio University study as unsound, and felt that the investigators approached the study with preconceived and negative conclusions. But the study was an inherently difficult one, and the results could hardly be other than inconclusive. Campbell and Erlebacher have demonstrated synthetically that regression artifacts alone could explain all the apparently trivial effects of Head Start, and strong cases can be made for the impact of other criticisms noted above. But it is also possible and arguable that Head Start participation *per se* can only have a minimal academic impact.

Present efforts to improve evaluations are largely directed toward solutions of statistical and quantitative artifacts. These difficulties *do* often eviscerate the value of evaluation efforts, and it is conceivable that sophisticated techniques will become available to transcend these problems. But rather little attention has been directed to the *context* of social evaluations. Ultimately in the present political climate the decision about the impact of a social program evaluation is made on political rather than on scientific grounds. Massive programs may be funded in order apparently to authenticate a commitment to the disadvantaged, on the one hand, or may be undercut because they tend to grate on powerful political interests, on the other, and each with hardly any consideration of the efficacy of the program itself for the intended recipients [13].

To the extent to which our armament includes the capacity to apply powerful and even-handed statistical techniques to social program evaluations without our appreciating the rather more inequitable political environment in which the statistical measures are being applied and interpreted—to that extent we are equally likely to exacerbate a problem as to supply a solution.

We have discussed in some detail the "latent conservative function" of evaluation findings and the ways in which positive findings tend to preserve the status quo. However, as is true with any politically volatile program, there are those who *fear* a program being evaluated in a positive light. The following conversation held on May 25, 1972, with Chichard Cheney of the Cost of Living Council amplifies this point:

> OEO has recently really cracked down on their evaluations. This is especially true of the evaluation of the Performance Contracting Experiment. The hypothesis was that, by bringing incentive-oriented U.S. enterprise into the education game, the kids would be the ultimate winners through better curricula, techniques, etc. The theory was that competition in educational programs would improve their quality. . . . The politics of this are very interesting. The American Federation of Teachers raised hell about the experiment when it was in the formative stages. They attempted to have OEO funds earmarked so that the experiment could not be done. The House Education and Labor Committee was approached by AFT; they tried to get them to write language into law so that the experiment could not be done.

We can infer that the education lobby feared the introduction of capitalist incentive techniques into their domain—further evidence that evaluation is a political issue, depending both upon the perspective and values of the viewer and upon whether or not the results are perceived as negative or positive.

THE ENVIRONMENT FOR EVALUATION: FACTORS THAT IMPEDE

This section identifies both the political and non-political factors that have a tendency to impede the successful completion of evaluation research. The theme for the section (as well as for the case study of OFC) is the contrast between ideal evaluation research and the actual situation with all its constraints. At least two dimensions to this problem deserve special emphasis. First, there is the question of flexibility. Given the nature of the different goals and interests of program administrators and evaluators, what are the limits of "reasonable" or "flexible" behavior on the part of both sides as opposed to "unreasonable" or "inflexible" behavior? Second, what barriers to evaluation research are caused by misunderstandings between the parties (which can presumably be rectified through education efforts toward both sides as to the role and needs of the other) and what barriers are caused by deliberate sabotage (the impeding of the research effort by operations people or by the evaluation team for political or selfish motives)? These implications are explored in later sections of the book.

Non-Political Barriers to Evaluation Research

Administrators resent the intrusion of evaluators because they take time that their operating people could use more advantageously to solve day-to-day agency problems. In addition, the methodologies are often imperfect; and the measuring instruments poor. Much careful work is involved in credible evaluation research, but measurement error can occur through unreliability of indices, confounding with other concepts unintentionally included in an index. respondent confusion or hostility, deliberate fabrication, equipment error, or simply the trivialization of a complex concept with a simple index.

According to Evans, evaluation in particular and social science in general is a foreign way of thinking to most politicians and administrators who typically do not come from social or physical science backgrounds. This mode of thinking is a result of formal scientific training.[14] To further compound the problem, social scientists themselves have a limited interest in evaluation. The socialization process of graduate school produces a bias toward "pure" or laboratory research and against practical or applied careers, which thus reduces the number and probably the quality of social scientists engaged in applied social science research.[15]

The social researcher rarely has control of the research situation. Factors beyond the researcher's control intervene to reduce the potency or credibility of the findings. Pitfalls to interpretation have been categorized in a variety of ways, of which the most widely known and influencial are those of Campbell and Stanley: threats to internal validity and to external validity [16] Threats to internal validity: In the search for a causal relationship, these are the threats which might cause us falsely to believe that a causal relationship exists. These threats include the following:

1. *History*—events, other than the experimental treatment, occurring between pretest and post-test and thus providing an alternate explanation of effects;
2. *Maturation*—processes within the respondents or observed social units producing changes as a result of the passage of time per se;
3. *Instability*—unreliability of measures, fluctuations in sampling persons or components, autonomous instability of repeated or "equivalent" measures;
4. *Testing*—the effect of taking a test on the scores of the second test;

5. *Instrumentation*—changes in the calibration of a measuring instrument or changes in the observers or scores used may produce changes in the obtained measurements;
6. *Regression Artifacts*—pseudoshifts occurring when persons or treatment units have been selected on the basis of their extreme scores;
7. *Selection*—biases resulting from differential recruitment of comparison groups, producing different mean levels on the measure of effect;
8. *Experimental Mortality*—the differential loss of respondents from comparison groups;
9. *Selection-Maturation Interaction*—selection biases resulting in differential rates of "maturation" or autonomous change.

Cook and Campbell [17] have recently added other threats to internal validity which have particular relevance for treatments in political environments:

10. *Diffusion or Imitation of Treatment*—Where treatment groups and no treatment control or comparison groups are in communication with one another directly, or indirectly through the media, the controls may in fact receive the treatment or some part of it and thereby be rendered inappropriate for comparison.
11. *Compensatory Equalization of Treatment*—To provide equity where the assignment of some persons to receive no treatment is politically or morally unacceptable, alternate treatments are sometimes administered to controls, making statistical comparison difficult.
12. *Compensatory Rivalry*—Again, where one's assignment to treatment or control group is known, competitive compensation among the controls invalidates the comparison between treatment and control conditions.
13. *Local History*—Since treatments are not uniformly administered in the same place, and since place and conditions of place are sometimes confounded with treatment, particularly in policy generated treatments, these irrelevant local events may look like treatment effects.

Threats to external validity: Once a causal relationship between treatment and outcome is known, one is also concerned with the generalizability of the causal relationship across times and settings. To the extent that the finding is attributable to the conditions of a particular experimental setting never likely to be duplicated, public policy based on the finding may be misguided. Threats to external validity include the following: [18]

1. *Interaction Effects of Testing*—the effect of a pretest in increasing or decreasing the respondent's sensitivity or responsiveness to the experimental variable, thus making the results unrepresentative;

2. *Interaction of selection and experimental treatment*—unrepresentative responsiveness of the treated population;
3. *Reactive Effects of Experimental Arrangements*—"artificiality"—conditions making the experimental setting atypical;
4. *Multiple Treatment Interference*—where multiple treatments are jointly applied, effects atypical of the separate application of the treatments;
5. *Irrelevant Responsiveness of Measures*—all measures are complex and all include irrelevant components that may produce apparent effects;
6. *Irrelevant Replicability of Treatments*—treatments are complex and replications of them may fail to include those components actually responsible for the effects.

To these, Cook and Campbell have added yet another critical set of threats to validity, under the general categories of *conclusion validity* and *construct validity.* [19]

Threats to Conclusion Validity: Necessary for inferring a causal relationship is the demonstration that the treatment (cause) and effect co-vary. Threats to conclusion validity exist when statistical conditions of co-variation *falsely* lead us to conclude that a cause-effect relationship has (or has not) been established. These threats, a subset of internal validity issues, include:

1. *Statistical Power*—an error resulting from small sample size, inappropriate criteria for rejecting the null-hypothesis, and related statistical issues.
2. *Fishing and the Error Rate Problem*—treating multiple statistical comparisons on the same data as if they were independent of one another.
3. *Reliability of Measures*—measures of low reliability which inflate error terms and force inappropriate acceptance of the null hypothesis.
4. *Reliability of Treatment Implementation*—unstandardized implementations across persons or across occasions which inflate error variances.
5. *Random Irrelevancies in the Experimental Setting*—uncontrolled aspects of a treatment setting which increase error variances.
6. *Random Heterogeneity of Respondents*—inevitable and irrelevant differences among respondents introduce variances which mask or suppress treatment effects.

Threats to Construct Validity: Once a finding is established statistically, or a cause-effect relationship known, one still might inappropriately conceptualize or label a cause and/or effect, so that incorrect generalizations occur and misleading lessons are learned. In some ways this list is a reworking of threats to external validity (a case study in construct validity!), but the issues deserve separate treatment here. Some of these threats are particularly relevant to our concerns, and include:

1. *Operationalizations Which Underrepresent the Construct*—measuring work satisfaction through noting rates of absenteeism, for example, and then equating the two.
2. *Generalizing Across Time*—measuring an outcome at a particular time, properly noting a causal treatment, and then inappropriately assuming that the treatment would cause the outcome at a different time.
3. *Experimenter Expectancies*—cause-effect relationships between variables which exist only because the experimenter acts (often inadvertantly) to cause the outcome. Properly understood, the expectancies are (or are part of) the treatment.
4. *Reactive Arrangements*—persons responding to an experimental treatment but only because they know they are in an experimental situation.
5. *Confounding Constructs and Levels of Constructs*—administering a low level treatment which has no impact, for example, and assuming that the treatment would not work at any level.
6. *Resentful Demoralization of Controls*—savvy no-treatment subjects who perform at a lower than normal level, which in statistical comparison makes the treatment look like a success.

One can see how these categories are exemplified in the drug-research and management training examples from chapter 2, and in the Head Start discussion of this chapter. In reality these issues are never satisfactorily dealt with in the most pristine scientific endeavors. They plague the field researcher even more, and provide an impossible standard for the researcher whose efforts occur in complex and controversial political environments.

Statistical devices are being developed which attempt to compensate for some of these problems. But it is clear that many of the threats above are not amenable to statistical treatment. Since it is also apparent that some of the difficulties assert themselves with particular tenacity in the social action—social amelioration environments which are the primary concern of this book, it is especially important that administrators and practitioners be aware of these issues in order to blunt their impact where possible, and to recognize the alternative explanations of findings which they often provide.

Additional Political Barriers to Evaluation Research

As mentioned previously, the role of the program administrator and the role of the objective evaluator naturally conflict. The program administrator is necessarily a program advocate under the present system, because if he/she reports to Congress that the program is not working, the administrator is often blamed. Program failure becomes equated with personal failure.

In addition, an honest evaluation will tend to indict an incompetent administrator. The public availability of scientific evidence that attests to the failure of a program can be an embarrassment. Therefore, both inept administrators who know their programs fail because of personal incompetence, and good administrators who know they are failing because of the insurrmountable nature of the problem they are tackling will tend to resist even-handed evaluations in the present political climate. Since the decision to hire an evaluation team often rests with agency policymakers, evaluations may only proceed once "reasonable assurance" of favorable evaluation outcomes is obtained in advance.

Since the funding of evaluations often comes from operational funds which can be diverted to other purposes, this too can impede effective evaluations. Often, for example, the monies set aside for an evaluation, which can be ruinous to an administrator, can be utilized instead for an information system of some kind. The information in the system may be totally defined for administrative purposes and therefore be useless for evaluation in some larger sense, but nevertheless satisfy the evaluation requirements of most observers.[20]

Agency resources usually are limited, and any new commitment, especially one with a distant payoff (if indeed any payoff), is viewed as a drain on these resources.[21] An agency with limited funds can realistically be expected to concentrate on administrative commitments. In fact, just to insure that evaluations are conducted, Congress has instructed federal agencies to set aside 1 percent of their funds to be used explicitly for program evaluation.

Evaluation research in particular and social science research in general also can be used as a substitute for real action. The cry of "We don't have enough information to complete the analysis" can be a subterfuge for general also can be used as a substitute for real action. The cry of "We don't have enough information to complete the analysis" can be a subterfuge for "deep-sixing" a program. Social scientists traditionally are slow to assert that hypotheses are supported or refuted. They often refuse to commit themselves to the validity of their field findings. In a similar vein, preliminary scientific findings (such as from a demonstration pilot project) can be used as a politically expedient way to back out of programs that are viewed as undesirable. For example, the New Jersey Graduated Income Tax Experiment was seen by some as political fuel for the Nixon Administration to revamp the existing welfare program.

Many agency administrators, because of their commitment to—and ego-involvement with their programs, assume that the programs work and do not see the need for an evaluation of something they already know. An outcome of this orientation is that if an evaluation is initiated, it is designed to show that "everything works" rather than showing that some programs are better than others. Administrators, because of their vested interests in a program (i.e., their job, their reputation, their whole career) are "socialized" into taking the worthwhileness of their program(s) for granted, even if they were not involved in the actual program design.[22]

Because of opposition by program administrators (who are influential in the resource allocation process within the agency), evaluation often receives a limited resource and funding commitment.[23] If the evaluation then proves negative, the administrator can say that the study was performed in a less than "scientifically sound" manner. The Congressional requirement that 1 percent of total agency funds go to evaluation research represents an attempt to deal with this problem.

Frequently, administrators are convinced that evaluation research is not really scientific and cannot be relied upon to produce valid and reliable results.[24] They are fearful of negative results which, they feel, might be due to evaluator error or biases. They are understandably reluctant to risk their careers on some technique they do not even trust. Also, especially with poverty-type social action programs, administrators have had bad experiences with academic researchers. These "objective researchers" have come in, have taken up their time, and have departed, rarely helping with their problems in any way. Moreover, the research (if it were even slightly negative) hindered them greatly in their funding request for the next fiscal period. Academicians have frequently entered a community, asked a few embarrassing questions, and promised some vague and future benefit from the research, [which is scarcely forthcoming, especially in the short term].[25] Furthermore, the projects are often undertaken at the expense of the community's short-term goals.

One political problem seems to be generic to social action programs.[26] No matter what social action strategy is implemented, the evaluation is to provide about the program. The assumption is that improvement necessarily will follow proper research. However, this assumption ignores the reality of the political and economic situation. Poverty is functional for the nonpoor.[27] It can be hypothesized that the powerful and wealthy are well entrenched and resistant to social change efforts. Highly placed politicos often seem to be too enmeshed in politically beneficial "deals" to support full disclosure. One might submit that social action programs are doomed to failure because they rarely have the full support of powerful people and institutions. In this environment, trivially financed and ill-backed evaluations will only serve to document failure, destroy illusions, and aggravate frustrations.[28]

Bureaucratic structures tend to perpetuate themselves. The goals of a bureaucracy are survival, stability, power, and growth. These goals may conflict with the programs' goals (especially if the program goals are aimed at the elimination of a problem, as Campbell suggests in *Reforms as Experiments*). If the evaluation says the program is solving the problem for which it was established, it may be perceived that there is a danger the organization will put itself out of business; organization pressures then will force either a poor performance (for a poor evaluation next time) or the seeking of a new problem area to justify the organization's continued existence. In any event, if the results of the evaluation weaken the organization's power, it will be met by covert and/or overt resistance.

One large source of political problems with evaluation lies in the conflict between the policy level and the operations level of an organization. Evaluation research usually is supported most strongly, if it is supported at all, by those in policymaking positions who face questions about the allocation of resources among programs.[29] These policymakers want some "proof" of the efficacy of their decisions; evaluation results can provide the needed support. However, policymakers often are reluctant or powerless to enforce conditions on operating units (especially when different levels of government are involved) that are essential for sound research. It is at the operating level that data are collected, information stored, and services provided. It is also the people at the operating level (including the agency administrator) who have the most to lose from a negative evaluation.

In initial definition and in evaluation implementation, they are subject to pressures and counterpressures from congressional committees, interest groups, professional guilds and the public. They often are caught up in interagency and intra-agency maneuvering for advantage and influence.[30] The following examples show how the political features of programs can complicate the conduct of evaluation research.

Program Goals. Evaluations ideally should start from the goals of the program. Since the purpose is to compare observed effects with intended effects, program goals should be clear, concise, and measurable. This is rarely the case. In the Westinghouse study, for example, one of the criticisms was that the study was too narrow because it did not encompass *all* the goals of Head Start. How does one measure an increase in community involvement that comes about because of Head Start?

Goals generally are global, diffuse, and diverse. Coalition support often is required so that adoption of a program can be secured. Many different values and interests must be won over, and consequently a host of unrealistic promises are made in the guise of program goals. Diffuse and unmeasurable goals inhibit evaluation. In addition, it is often difficult to ascertain which goals are real and which are merely window dressing. Actors at different levels in the system perceive and interpret goals in different ways. The evaluator is faced with the dual task of sifting the real from the unreal, the overt from the covert, the important from the unimportant, as well as of discerning the priorities among goals. Failing this, he will evaluate the program against meaningless criteria.[31]

Historically, evaluation studies have had little impact on agency policymaking. One reason for this is that only official goals have been addressed. Evaluations have ignored the non-instrumental goals that programs serve. Perhaps if important latent goals were also identified, one might learn more about the program's real successes. Latent goals might be those that would show the administration was "doing something" like placating powerful interest groups or enhancing the influence of a particular group vis-a-vis another. One might thus better understand why some policies survive despite terrible evaluations, why some programs rate high on some indicators of goal achievement and are nevertheless abandoned, and which factors have the most influence on the making and the persistence of policy.[32]

There is no question that a case can be made for multiple-goal evaluation. With single goals, refunding of the agency rests upon a narrowly defined "success" criterion, which makes it difficult for the administrator to cooperate with the evaluator. He may either manipulate the indicators or in some other way insure a favorable outcome. To make matters worse, the techniques used for evaluating goal achievement are generally poor at best. Imprecise working definitions and indices often are used. Similarly, a poor understanding frequently exists concerning the relationship between program activities and ultimate agency goals. While non-quantitative goal measurement is equally important (but extremely difficult to accomplish), researchers sometimes opt for "safe" quantitative measures. The truth of the matter is that some projects cannot be evaluated properly in their present climate, or with the present skills and tools; such a situation may insure the fabrication of results.[33]

While single-goal evaluations generally are perceived as inadequate by researchers, there is little agreement on what should be done in the face of goal diversity and lack of clarity.[34] Some argue that a broad-aim program with multiple objectives is inherently unsuitable for experimental evaluation.[35] As an alternative, process evaluation is suggested. A process evaluation collects qualitative as well as quantitative data, thereby focusing upon a complete description of events as they develop through time. In other words, a case study approach to evaluation research is seen as superior to the familiar hypothesis-testing approach.

It can be hypothesized that evaluation research that has influenced policy is more likely to have been done in the process tradition than in the experimental tradition. However, process evaluation is in disrepute with most evaluation researchers.[36] If utility is weighed equally with validity, this value judgment may be too harsh. Descriptive studies seem appropriate to programs that lack clearly specified goals and have inadequate data bases; they may provide information to help clarify these points at some future time. More specifically, process analysis can help a researcher clarify the goals and accomplishments of a particular program, determine the salient alternatives, and, in the interim, feed valuable information to agency policymakers.

It has been suggested that decision making in situations where there is agreement on well-defined goals should differ from situations where such agreement is lacking.[37] In a well-structured problem, optimal decisions can perhaps be aided through use of a sophisticated methodology that is derived from statistical decision theory. Lacking goal agreement, such a methodology is inappropriate. The implications of this situation for evaluation research are twofold. First, as the ease of identifying objectives varies from area to area, so does the type of methodology that is feasible and appropriate. Second, clarity and degree of agreement upon program goals affect not only the type of evaluation methodology that is appropriate, but also the likelihood that evaluation results will eventually feed into the policy process. If a program has multiple goals and the evaluation focuses on one or a subset of these, the policymaker who relies on statistical evidence can easily and legitimately reject its conclusion (as was seen in the Westinghouse experiment).

In our earlier listing and discussion of threats to validity as enumerated by Campbell and others, some threats were rather more salient than others to the case study which is the primary focus of this book. To conclude this chapter we shall briefly touch again on those issues of particular concern to us here.

Variations in Program Inputs.   It is often assumed that all local operationalizations of social action programs are similar to one another, or that the local differences are to be treated as error variances for statistical purposes. With this assumption, national impact projections may be developed from the data. But this is normally a falacious assumption in a political context, for local variations in implementation and measurement strategy may be among the most critical data.[38] The perusal of total impact evaluation figures may mask important variations; sites, strategy mixes, or modes of operation may differ completely. This is crucial information and the researcher should ask the question "Under what conditions is the program likely to be successful?" A methodology of evaluation research should first and foremost be sensitive to the political and social nature of the environment within which it must be conducted.

Program Changes.   Political considerations directly affect the stability of programs. Within brief time periods, programs often are forced to shift activities, objectives, and/or strategies. They respond to changes in administration, legislation, policy, ideology, financial liberality, and the like. For the evaluator, such changes represent threats to the research. If the evaluator is to persist with the original measures of program effectiveness, these measures may become irrelevant to a changed program focus. Even if the original indicators remain relevant, to what can the researcher attribute the observed effects? To the original program? To the changed program? To the shift from the one to the other? As will be seen in the OFC case study, this problem loomed large for evaluators of the OFC experiments.

Randomization.   A crucial feature of an evaluation study which incorporates the most profound characteristics of laboratory social science is the random assignment of subjects to treatment and control groups. In fact, many of the threats to validity noted above assume this random assignment and focus on distortions in an otherwise randomized experiment. But more often than not a social action context randomization is given lip service at best and then slighted for administrative reasons. Researchers may wish, for example, to assign participants randomly to experimental groups, only to have legislators decide that equity requires that all subjects receive equal (and often unevaluable) treatment. Failing that, they may want to reserve for themselves the decision about which subjects (or constituents) receive treatment. Administrators want to retain the authority to allocate programs to agencies. Staff members usually want to exercise their judgment in accepting individuals for treatment. All these constraints usually eliminate the possibility of true randomization.

Academicians traditionally are very naive in the political arena. As a consequence, the research designs created by academic social scientists make demands that exceed real-world realities. Because of a "pure research" bias and a concomitant paramount concern for precision of measurement and analysis, academics are often paralyzed when it comes to dealing with typically ambiguous social environments.

Administrator Responses to the Political Environment

The political effects on an evaluation study can range from the merely annoying to the disastrous. Program managers, local directors, and staff may refuse to allow access to information and/or to people, or they may refuse to allow control groups or subvert them. Their record-keeping may be incomplete or faulty, or they may manipulate the data that provide indicators of success. In many cases, the researcher may be promised support so that the agency may receive the legitimacy and publicity that "scientific evaluations" offer. However, once the researcher's task begins, deceit, duplicity, and non-cooperation are encountered. Crucial or potentially damaging data are often removed or subverted. In contrast, evaluators may be received with open arms if the administrator *knows* the result of the evaluation will be positive. A good example of this is a study of the Chicago Board of Education and the racial imbalance, if any, of public school expenditures.[39] The Chicago Board knew an imbalance would be found, but the members also knew they could not be blamed for it. They knew the imbalance in per pupil expenditures was a result of the higher-paid white teachers (who had more seniority than the typical black teachers) being concentrated, according to *their own placement requests*, in white schools. Full evaluative cooperation by an agency can mean that the agency knows well in advance what the results will be.[40]

The "trapped administrator", because of the political dilemma, often chooses various techniques to insure favorable evaluations. One technique is to choose the worst year and the worst social unit as guidelines. There is nowhere to go but up.[41] Another method is to secure vocal testimonials from those who have received the experimental treatment.[42] Still a third ploy is the confounding of selection and treatment. The trick is to select the more able subjects and insure that they are well-placed in the treatment group. This insures bias.[43] Ambiguity, lack of truly comparable bases for comparison, and lack of concrete evidence all work to increase the administrator's control over what gets said or at least to reduce the bite of criticism in the event of actual failure.

From the foregoing, it is easy to see how difficult it is to conduct "objective" evaluation research in a complex social environment. They provide a framework, a comparison for the experiences of one social action program and its evaluation.

The next chapter describes the historical and economic contexts within which OFC was thrust during the evolution of minority economic development interests in the United States. It is within these contexts that its evaluation can best be understood.

NOTES

1. John W. Evans and Walter Williams, "The Politics of Evaluation: The Case of Head Start," *Annals of the American Journal for Political and Social Science* (September 1969), p. 375.
2. Noralou P. Roos, "Evaluation, Quasi-Experimentation and Public Policy: Observations by a Short-Term Bureaucrat," in J.A. Camposaro and L.L. Roos, Jr. (eds.), *Quasi-Experiments: Testing Theory and Evaluating Policy* (Evanston, Ill.: Northwestern University Press, 1973), p. 4.
3. For a complete discussion of this phenomenon, see Charles Hampden-Turner, "The Philosophy of Science," an unpublished manuscript written for the Center for Community Economic Development, Cambridge, Massachusetts (1972), p. 26.
4. See Sar Levitan, *Federal Aid to Depressed Areas* (Baltimore: Johns Hopkins Press, 1964) for a vivid description of the problems of goal setting with the Area Redevelopment Act.
5. Donald T. Campbell, "Reforms as Experiments," *Urban Affairs Quarterly* (December 1971), p. 164.
6. Ibid., p. 134.
7. Reginald K. Carter, "Client's Resistance to Negative Findings and the Latent Conservative Function of Evaluation Studies," *The American Sociologist* (May 1971), p. 119.
8. Ibid., p. 122.
9. Evans and Williams, "The Politics of Evaluation."
10. Ibid., p. 308.
11. See Donald L. Campbell and A. Erlebacher, "How Regression Artifacts in Quasi-Experimental Evaluations Can Mistakenly Make Compensatory Education Look Harmful," in D. Hellmuth (ed.), *Compensatory Education: A National Debate* (New York: Brunner-Mazel, 1970).

12. Evans and Williams, "The Politics of Evaluation," p. 388.
13. Andrew C. Gordon, "University-Community Relations: Problems and Prospects," in *Cities in Change: Studies on the Urban Condition,* John Walton and Donald E. Carns, eds. (Boston: Allyn & Bacon, 1973), pp. 559–561.
14. John W. Evans, "Evaluating Social Action Programs," *Social Science Qtr.,* Vol. 50 (Dec. 1969), pp. 568–569.
15. Ibid., p. 570.
16. Donald T. Campbell and Julian C. Stanley, *Experimental and Quasi-Experimental Designs for Research* (Chicago: Rand-McNally, 1963), pp. 137–9.
17. Thomas P. Cook and Donald T. Campbell, "The Design and Conduct of Quasi-Experiments and True Experiments in Field Settings," to appear in M.D. Dunette (ed.), *Handbook of Industrial and Organizational Research.*
18. Campbell and Stanley, pp. 137–9.
19. Cook and Campbell.
20. See Andrew C. Gordon, Stanley W. Diverulie, Margaret T. Gordon and Jack Heinz, "Public Information and Public Access: A Sociological Interpretation," *Northwestern University Law Review,* May–June, 1973, pp. 280–308.
21. Gordon, "University-Community Relations: Problems & Prospects," pp. 564–5.
22. Edward A. Suchman, *Evaluative Research* (New York: Russell Sage Foundation, 1968), p. 147.
23. Ibid., p. 22.
24. Ibid., p. 147.
25. Gordon, "University-Community Relations: Problems and Prospects," p. 558.
26. Ibid., pp. 20–21.
27. See Herbert J. Gans, "The Uses of Poverty: The Poor Pay All," *Social Policy* (July–August 1971) and William Ryan, *Blaming the Victim* (New York: Vintage Books, 1971).
28. Gordon, "University-Community Relations: Problems and Prospects," pp. 564–566.
29. Carol H. Weiss, "The Politics of Evaluation," paper presented to the Annual Meeting of the Midwest Political Science Association, Chicago, Illinois, p. 3.
30. Ibid.
31. Ibid., p. 5.
32. Ibid., p. 6.
33. Gordon, "University-Community Relations: Problems and Prospects."
34. Roos, "Evaluation, Quasi-Experimentation and Public Policy," p. 17.
35. Robert S. Weiss and Martin Rein, "The Evaluation of Broad Aim Programs: Difficulties in Experimental Design and an Alternative," in C.H. Weiss (ed.), *Evaluating Action Programs* (Boston: Allyn & Bacon, 1972).

36. Roos, "Evaluation, Quasi-Experimentation and Public Policy," p. 14.
37. See Raymond Mack, *Planning on Uncertainty: Decision Making in Business and Government Administration* (New York: John Wiley and Sons, 1971).
38. Carol H. Weiss, "The Politics of Evaluation," p. 6.
39. Richard Berk, Raymond Mack, and John McKnight, "Race and Class Differences in Per Pupil Expenditure in Chicago, 1969–70," *Northwestern University Center for Urban Affairs* (1971).
40. Gordon, "University-Community Relations: Problems and Prospects," pp. 559–560.
41. Campbell, "Reforms as Experiments," p. 145.
42. Ibid., p. 164.
43. Ibid., p. 165.

Chapter Four

OFC in the Federal Context of Minority Economic Development

Federal programs designed specifically to assist in minority enterprise development are relatively recent. Minority enterprise development as a new thrust was initiated in the mid-1960s, growing to major program proportions during the early 1970s. However, the federal government has been involved in a variety of programs that aim to improve jobs, education, housing, and health opportunities for minorities* for more than five decades. Much of this effort during the past decade has been directed toward removing the discriminatory job barriers existing for minority workers. During the late 1960s, federal involvement in anti-discrimination efforts led quite naturally to more affirmative and larger scale programs in job recruitment, training, and placement.

Government anti-discrimination programs have been initiated in three distinct ways. First, some programs are based on the power of the executive branch of the government to contract and to use this contracting power to ensure that federal contractors do not discriminate in hiring or upgrading. This executive power has been used to require more than mere non-discrimination, and programs of affirmative action are now required of virtually all federal government contractors. The second force in the development of federal programs is legislative in nature. It began at the federal level with the Civil Rights Act of 1964, and stems from the constitutional power of Congress to regulate interstate commerce.[1] The third source of influence derives from decisions of the U.S. Supreme Court from 1868 to the present, that require non-discrimination in a variety of economic endeavors. These decisions are based on pro-

*For the purposes of this book we recognize three major minority groupings: *Non-whites* (blacks and Asian Americans); *native Americans* (Aleuts, Eskimos, Hawaiians, and Indians); and *persons of Spanish-speaking ancestry* (Cubans, Mexicans, Puerto Ricans, and other persons of Latin American extraction). Asian American is broken down into four categories—Chinese, Filipino, Japanese, and others. In total, these minority groups comprise slightly over 17 percent of the American population or about 36 million people in the 1970 census.

visions of the Fourteenth Amendment to the Constitution and require that the "privileges and immunities" of citizens of the United States shall not be abridged and that "due process" and "equal protection" of the laws be accorded all citizens.

The efforts of the federal government to promote minority enterprise have taken the form of direct grants, loans, loan guarantees, and the purchase of goods and services. The government has also attempted to stimulate non-minority business investment and technical assistance for minority enterprise development through exhortations to civic duty by various administration members. Very few federal dollars, other than those provided indirectly in guarantees for bank loans, have actually been made available to help private sector firms stimulate their investment of monetary or technical resources in minority enterprise development.

Direct federal aid to minority enterprise, however, has grown dramatically since fiscal year (FY) 1969. The total of federal loans, loan guarantees, grants, and procurement was somewhat more than $200 million in FY 1969 (see Table 4-1). FY 1973 expenditures were more than $1.4 billion (see Table 4-2). The total federal program budget for this five-year period exceeds $3.4 billion with a growth rate of about 700 percent between FY's 1969 and 1973. Second only to law enforcement, this minority enterprise development program became the fastest growing domestic initiative of the Nixon Administration[2] and the only major initiative in minority development by that administration.

The monies allocated to aid minority enterprise are divided among programs in the following areas: (1) procurement—direct procurement by various federal agencies and the SBA administered "8(a)" procurement program; (2) loans—direct and guaranteed; (3) grants—technical assistance, public works and community development corporations (CDC's); and (4) construction—bonds minority contracting programs. Only about $250 million of the 1.4 billion FY 1973 total represents out-of-pocket costs because much of the $1.4 billion represents guarantee reserves in the U.S. Treasury or payment for goods and services that are needed by the government.

The relative success of these efforts in the enterprise area is very much in doubt, since no extensive evaluation has been made of the relative effectiveness of these programs. Furthermore, there have been no experimental programs implemented to provide feedback on effective methods of minority business development. Only OFC was initiated with the distinct mission of providing data from which minority enterprise programs can be modified and new programs started.

No judgment about the value or effectiveness of federal programs will therefore be made here. This chapter reviews briefly early state and federal efforts to protect minorities against job discrimination, Supreme Court decisions that gradually made discrimination in many areas of economic life illegal, federal legislation affirming the civil rights of minorities, and various federal government

Table 4–1. Summary of Fiscal Years 1969–1973: Federal Funds Obligated to Minority Business Development

Category	Fiscal Year 1969	Fiscal Year 1970	Fiscal Year 1971	Fiscal Year 1972	Fiscal Year 1973	Total
Financial Grants, Loans, and Loan Guarantees by Federal Agencies	$200,000,000	$315,236,045	$434,019,716	$472,617,473	$ 670,185,569	$2,090,058,803
8 (a) Procurement by Federal Agencies	8,884,141	21,814,292	66,120,409	151,598,150	207,954,732	456,371,724
Direct and Subcontract Procurement by Federal Agencies	3,972,365	8,220,042	77,863,045	242,254,264	523,516,566	855,826,282
Total	$212,856,506	$212,856,506	$578,003,170	$866,469,887	$1,401,565,867	$3,404,256,809

Source: Data provided by OMBE in October 1973

Table 4-2. Summary of Federal Funding for Minority Business Development, Fiscal Year 1973 (July 1, 1972–June 30, 1973)

Agency	8 (a) Procurement	Direct Procurement	Loans and Guarantees	Grants	Total
ACTION	$ 316,925	$ 1,433,217	—	$ 310,897	$ 2,061,039
Agriculture	1,557,138	765,491	$ 34,772,000	—	37,094,629
Atomic Energy Commission	882,426	6,491,000	—	—	7,373,426
Civil Service Commission	13,948	—	—	—	13,948
Commerce, Dept. of	4,906,479	24,476,360	8,338,193	29,594,718	67,315,750
Defense, Dept. of	104,819,270	unknown	—	—	104,819,270
EEOC	473,249	390,667	—	—	863,916
Executive Office of President	360,222	—	—	—	360,222
Environmental Protection Agency	1,091,481	6,100,000	—	—	7,191,481
General Accounting Office	6,000	—	—	—	6,000
General Services Administration	21,749,388	4,060,439	—	—	25,809,827
HEW, Dept. of	10,124,616	12,936,000	—	3,226,052	26,286,668
HUD, Dept. of	777,852	356,206,071	—	61,530,000	418,513,923
Interior, Dept. of	1,737,491	64,984,703	1,250,000	—	67,972,194
Justice, Dept. of	97,953	—	—	—	97,953
Labor, Dept. of	3,560,164	16,147,233	—	—	19,707,397
NASA	7,832,132	5,364,000	—	—	13,196,132
National Weather Service	40,411	—	—	—	40,411
OEO	2,038,146	1,892,000	—	61,922,340	65,852,486
Postal Service	(230,509)[a]	2,491,585	—	—	2,261,076
Redevelopment Land Agency	571,212	1,420,800	—	—	1,922,012
SBA	1,187,729	5,000,000[b]	464,264,369	4,977,000[c]	475,429,098
State Department	988,435	165,000	—	—	1,153,435
Transportation, Dept. of	30,545,204	2,719,500	—	—	33,264,704
Treasury, Dept. of	54,709	9,500	—	—	64,209
VA	12,429,661	10,463,000	—	—	22,892,661
Indian Claims Commission	10,000	—	—	—	10,000
Library of Congress	13,000	—	—	—	13,000
Total	$207,954,732	$523,516,566	$508,624,562	$161,561,007	$1,401,656,867

[a] Debit; added last year.
[b] XS 8(a) Costs.
[c] Call contract grants.
Source: Data provided by OMBE in October 1973

programs designed to improve job and enterprise opportunities for minorities. This material will provide background information for analyzing the role and operation of OFC in the context of federal minority economic development programs.

EARLY EMPHASIS: ANTI-DISCRIMINATION IN JOBS AND JOB TRAINING

Historically, the individual states have implemented their own separate anti-discrimination programs. The power given to state agencies to act in cases of discriminatory practice varied widely—from "persuasion" to actual affirmative action or legal restraint. On the national level, the first presidential order in this area was promulgated in 1941 by Franklin D. Roosevelt (#8802). Roosevelt acquiesced to the threat of the black labor leader A. Philip Randolph to cut off minority manpower to the war effort if discriminatory policies were not stopped by executive action. In 1944, due in part to Randolph's increasing pressure, the U.S. Supreme Court ruled in a landmark case that a union must perform "its statutory duty to represent non-union or minority union members of the craft without hostile discrimination, fairly, impartially and in good faith." [3]

Although long on principle, Executive Orders such as No. 8802 were short on procedures or power for implementation. A committee on Fair Employment Practice was set up, but it was virtually powerless: even if non-compliance were found, prosecution of the offender was a long, arduous process. Shortly before the federal Fair Employment Practices Committee expired in 1945, New York enacted a statute that was to become a model for similar state agencies. This statute required that

1. Discrimination, if shown, be considered a misdemeanor;
2. The injured party be given the right to recover damages resulting from the discrimination; and
3. A public agency be empowered to make a contract with a contractor to deduct a penalty from its fee because of discrimination.

Racial discrimination, however, remained common. State commissions often lacked the power of initiation: they could not seek out the discriminator on their own but had to wait until a formal complaint was filed by an aggrieved party. Even though some state commissions were empowered to make limited investigations of suspected discrimination, they did not often use this prerogative. Other problems contributing to the commissions' lack of effectiveness included poor intra-governmental cooperation, investigators' fear of adverse reaction by powerful corporate entities, inadequate budgets, and heavy responsibilities.

The first five years of federal fair employment practices, therefore, saw minorities make gains in the labor market, but some of these gains were attributable to the wartime manpower shortage. Employers, unable to find usable white manpower, often turned to minorities as a "last resort." One result of such "last-in-hiring" policies was often that minority individuals were the "first out" when manpower needs lessened after the war (see Table 4–3).

Minorities have historically been discriminated against in all levels of government—local, state, and national—as well as by private industry.[5] This discrimination has continued to the present time and is the basic reason for income disparity between the nation's minority and white populations rather than deficiencies in their education or training.[6] It is discrimination which is often responsible for the inferior education received by minorities in most areas of the country and, as a consequence, many minorities are disqualified from employment at all levels above unskilled labor. This is particularly true for higher-level jobs. The lack of education provides a convenient "out" for white employers. It is a matter of record that minority unemployment has

Table 4–3.   Unemployment Rates: 1949 to 1970 (Annual Averages)

Year	Negro and Other Races	White	Ratio: Negro and Other Races to White
1948	5.2	3.2	1.6
1949	8.9	5.6	1.6
1950	9.0	4.9	1.8
1951	5.3	3.1	1.7
1952	5.4	2.8	1.9
1953	4.5	2.7	1.7
1954	9.9	5.0	2.0
1955	8.7	3.9	2.2
1956	8.3	3.6	2.3
1957	7.9	3.8	2.1
1958	12.6	6.1	2.1
1959	10.7	4.8	2.2
1960	10.2	4.9	2.1
1961	12.4	6.0	2.1
1962	10.9	4.9	2.2
1963	10.8	5.0	2.2
1964	9.6	4.6	2.1
1965	8.1	4.1	2.0
1966	7.3	3.3	2.2
1967	7.4	3.4	2.2
1968	6.7	3.2	2.1
1969	6.5	3.2	2.0
1970	8.2	4.5	1.8
1971	9.9	5.4	1.8
1972	10.0	5.0	2.0
1973	8.9	4.3	2.1

Note: The unemployment rate is the percent unemployed in the civilian labor force.

Source: U.S. Department of Labor, Bureau of Labor Statistics, *Employment & Earnings* (January 1974).

averaged twice the level of white unemployment over the last 25 years from 1948 to 1973 (see Table 4-3).

A review of U.S. Supreme Court decisions affecting civil rights, documents the lengthy and continuing struggle against discrimination undertaken by minorities in the United States.[7] Prior to 1868, the inequality of minorities was affirmed in the courts. Despite the Emancipation Proclamation of 1863, the Thirteenth Amendment to the Constitution in 1865 and the Fourteenth Amendment ratified in 1868, minorities continued to be subject to strong racism in every area of their lives. This racism was reinforced by the courts under the "separate but equal" doctrine.

Beginning in the 1920s and continuing for a decade, the Supreme Court began, in isolated instances, to question segregation and to provide equal protection in the administration of justice. Then, in the period from 1938 to 1954, the courts moved to attack segregated education, housing, and transportation and to ensure enfranchisement as required by the Fourteenth Amendment to the Constitution.

From 1954 to 1973, the Supreme Court was very active in the civil rights area. Many decisions were made regarding public accommodations, fair trials, and housing. It was not until the decade of the 1960s, however, that the nation witnessed the first real use of federal judicial power in the area of fair employment practices. Prior to that time, state fair employment laws were the primary impetus to change and, as we have indicated, they were quite ineffective. In the case of *Colorado Anti-Discrimination Commission vs. Continental Airlines* (1963), the Supreme Court ruled that prohibition of racial discrimination in employment in interstate commerce (an area of employment traditionally closed to minorities) does not unduly burden such commerce.[8] In *Todd vs. Joint Apprenticeship Committee of Steel Workers of Chicago* (1963), the Court directed a union's apprenticeship committee to admit minorities as members and to employ them as apprentices.[9] And, finally, the Court compelled the Georgia State Dental Association to admit minorities as members in *Bell vs. Georgia Dental Association* (1964).[10] Clearly, the power of the Constitution was used to protect minorities as equal citizens rather than to affirm their minority status.

FEDERAL LEGISLATION AT LAST: THE CIVIL RIGHTS ACT (1964)

House Resolution 7152—the bill that was to become (with many changes) the Civil Rights Act of 1964—was introduced by Congressman Emanuel Celler on June 20, 1963. This bill was passed under the authority of Congress to regulate interstate commerce as defined in such cases as *Wickard v. Filburn,* 317 U.S. 111 (1942).

It includes a battery of substantive prohibitions found in the typical state anti-discrimination law. An important provision of Title VII of this act was the creation of the Equal Employment Opportunity Commission (EEOC). This five-member Commission was established to insure compliance with Title VII (Fair Employment) on the part of employers, employment agencies, unions, and community organizations. The EEOC has generally proven weak in enforcement: "After many political compromises, the Commission became a poor enfeebled thing . . . with the power to conciliate but not compel."[11] The Commission was authorized under Title VII to use only informal methods to resolve discrimination complaints; the act specifies "conference, conciliation, and persuasion" as methods to use to combat unfair employment practices. However, the Commission could ask the Attorney General to take a case to court to enforce Title VII. Private litigants bring suit under Section 706, but only after they had exhausted the relevant state and EEOC procedures. The EEOC was further limited because it lacked the power to subpoena witnesses for hearings.

Aside from the statutory limitations just cited, EEOC has suffered from political problems, considerable turnover in chairmen, innumerable staff problems, and a lack of sufficient budget.[12] As a result of these handicaps, the Commission has not been an aggressive "self-starter" in initiating action against discriminators and has attempted to take care of filed complaints with a vague conciliation process.

In an effort to increase the power of the Commission, a bill to extend EEOC's powers to issue cease and desist orders was passed in the 92nd Congress.[13] The bill also includes the power to go to court to enforce its guidelines without relying upon the Attorney General to take action.[14] However, it is too soon to determine whether these new EEOC powers will result in a fully effective anti-discrimination agency.

Not only has Congress acted to curb discrimination in employment under its power to regulate interstate commerce, but the Executive Branch has acted under its contract authority to require more "affirmative action."

AFFIRMATIVE ACTIONS—OFCC:
EXECUTIVE ORDER NO. 11246

Executive Order No. 11246, issued by President Lyndon B. Johnson on September 24, 1965, was the sixth in a series of equal employment orders issued by presidents concerning fair employment in government contracts. (These orders date back to that of President Roosevelt in 1941.)

In 1966, employers with Federal contracts (primarily defense and aerospace) employed an estimated 24 million Americans or approximately one-third of the total labor force. Executive Order No. 11246, in addition to prohibiting discrimination, requires that federal contractors take "affirmative action to insure that applicants are employed, and that employees are treated equally during employment without regard to their race, color or national origin." [15] This order provides for separately administered compliance programs, coordinated and supervised by the Secretary of Labor through the Office of Federal Contract Compliance (OFCC). Every federal agency employing contracts in their operation falls under the jurisdiction of the OFCC.

The OFCC concept was implemented by Secretary of Labor Willard Wirtz in 1966. Opting for direct enforcement instead of voluntarism, OFCC is considered to have been more effective in motivating fair employment practices among federal contractors than has the EEOC among industry generally. However, OFCC has been criticized by civil rights leaders for its failure to apply sanctions and penalties against major contractors to enforce its affirmative action regulations. Another criticism is that mere tokenism will "get the contractor off the hook," whereas the goal should be substantially greater integration.

VARIOUS MANPOWER TRAINING AND EMPLOYMENT SERVICES [16]

Two basic causes of inequality in employment are discrimination and disadvantages in terms of job preparation and training. Title VII of the Civil Rights Act and Executive Order No. 11246 both focus on discrimination. However, the elimination of employment discrimination is not enough. As a by-product of discrimination, minority members have not historically had the opportunity to prepare themselves adequately for many jobs, particularly in the skilled and professional areas. Federal programs designed to deal with this problem were initiated during the 1960s.

The U.S. Employment Service (USES), established in 1933 as a part of the Department of Labor, is the operational center of the government's manpower system: 2,000 local offices of state employment services provide job referral, counseling, and testing services while administering the various manpower programs of the government. Other federal manpower programs have, at times, operated in parallel with USES. The Concentrated Employment Program (CEP), a more recent Labor Department program for the disadvantaged, operates independently of USES. Civil rights leaders have criticized both of these programs because of their alleged failure to attack discrimination effectively by assisting minorities to obtain meaningful employment, employment with the opportunity for growth and development.

The Human Resources Development Program (HRD) was initiated in 1966 by USES to "provide intensive services for the chronically unemployed." These services are conducted at youth opportunity centers run by state employment services. "Out-reach" staff help the chronically disadvantaged through counseling at HRD centers. Other manpower programs include Neighborhood Youth Corps, Job Corps, New Careers, and Special Impact.

PRIVATE SECTOR PROGRAMS

The Manpower Development and Training Act (MDTA) of 1962 initially sought
a mix of institutional and on-the-job training (OJT) to upgrade minority competition for jobs. Its goal was to retrain "mature, experienced, family heads
who had been displaced by technological and economic change while providing
them with income to make the training possible."

The most widely known program to come from MDTA is the
NAB–JOBS program. This program is administered by the Labor Department
in cooperation with the Commerce Department and the National Alliance for
Businessmen (NAB) and was initially headed by Henry Ford II. The purpose
of the program is to train the hard-core unemployed for work in private industry.
The initial target was 100,000 disadvantaged women and men on the job by
June 1969, and 500,000 by June 1971.

In the NAB–JOBS program an individual company may negotiate
with the Labor Department for a NAB–JOBS contract to provide remedial
training for hard-core unemployed, or a company may simply make a pledge
of a number of jobs for the hard-core and may pay for any special training
required. This latter approach avoids any special reporting to the government
as required by the manpower training contracts and avoids the necessity of
hiring only those applicants who are cleared by government interviewers. The
government pays the fixed unit costs plus an incentive award for each trainee
who is employed for longer than twelve months.

The business response to NAB–JOBS was a surprise; 40 percent of
the firms contacted made pledges. However, it soon became apparent that
getting pledges was one thing, turning them into job orders and placements was
something else. With 200,000 pledges in hand by October 1968, only 68,000
actual job openings had been offered and only 29,000 had been placed. A number of commentators have given the NAB program poor marks, and one 1970
report showed that the MA–5 program had employee retention rates of 40
percent and below in most cities.[17] This report also concluded that the
disadvantaged who were hired would probably have been hired regardless of
the NAB–JOBS commitment. However, this conclusion must be weighed against
the formidable measurement problems associated with determining the effectiveness of such a program. Some recent improvements in the JOBS program
(i.e., greater use of contract funds by employers, upgraded assistance by the
government and easing of financing arrangements) are designed to increase the
program's efficiency.

None of the work in the jobs area has focused on the development
of skills specifically tailored to enterprise development. It has been assumed
that providing job training and employment opportunities would somehow
mesh with the more recent emphasis on minority economic development through
minority enterprise. But there has been little or no attempt to systematically
relate the operations of the two programs.

FEDERAL SHIFT IN EMPHASIS

Despite the massive social legislation of the Johnson Era, minorities continued to suffer substantial economic and social disadvantages in 1968. Programs such as NAB-JOBS and OFCC plus commissions such as EEOC had not produced the instant success hoped for by the Johnson administration.

The new president, Richard M. Nixon, decided to make a switch in emphasis from anti-discrimination efforts in jobs and job training to what became known as "black capitalism" and later assumed the more general title of "minority capitalism." President Nixon pledged to provide not only jobs but greater wealth-creating opportunities for minorities, and less welfare. To understand the nature of the task undertaken by the Nixon Administration, it is necessary to examine the environment of minority enterprise development in some detail.

RATIONALE FOR A FEDERAL ROLE IN MINORITY ECONOMIC DEVELOPMENT

There are at least two reasons for federal involvement in minority economic development. The first is economic in nature, and the second reason is psychological. Both will be discussed.

Nature and Status of Minority Business Enterprise

From an economic point of view, a definite inequality of ownership of resources exists between minorities and non-minorities in the United States. The 17 percent of the population who are native American, black, Asian, or of Spanish-speaking ancestry control only a tiny fraction of the productive resources of the nation. The most recent census of all minority business ownership (1969) showed that about 322,000 business enterprises in this country were owned by minority group members. This represents about 4.3 percent of total U.S. enterprises (7,489,000).[18] Gross sales for these 322,000 businesses totaled $10.6 billion, or about 0.7 percent of the total $1,498 billion receipts figure for all U.S. business.[19] Thus the average minority business had sales of just under $33,000, while the average non-minority firm had sales of just under $182,000. This $10.6 billion sales figure was approximately equal to the sales of *one* non-minority firm, General Electric.

Contributing to the picture is the nature of many of these minority-owned enterprises. Of all minority businesses, 61 percent are either small retail or service establishments, largely lacking in capital assets. The businesses in these two categories account for 62 percent of all sales of minority businesses.[20] No minority business is included in the *Fortune* listing of the 500 largest American corporations, and the sales of the largest minority firm, Motown Industries, were about one-fifth those of the smallest of the 500 largest domestic corporations (Varian Associates, $204 million sales).[21] As such, minority control of capital is only a fractional amount of their 4 percent of business ownership. It has been estimated that minority businesses account for only about 0.3 percent of all business assets or about $2.6 billion out of the total U.S. business non-financial (corporate) assets of $859 billion in 1971.[22]

The statistics for financial institutions, the backbone of economic development, reflect the same kind of unequal distribution of economic resources. The combined assets of all minority banks, and the combined assets of all minority-owned insurance companies are about $2.6 billion, or less than 0.2 percent of the industry total of $1,607 billion.[23]

The continuing disparity of personal capital accumulation has significantly hampered the development of the economy of the minority community as well as the opportunities for enterprise development by individuals. The average minority family has assets of $3,398 as opposed to $19,612 for the non-minority family.[24] In 1970, the average minority family income was about 66 percent that of white family income, or about $6,650. While this represents a substantial relative income gain during the decade of the sixties, this gain was very unevenly distributed so that the lowest 20 percent of the minority population actually fell further behind during the sixties.[25] There was little gain in realtive unemployment rates, which were close to the historic level of twice those of non-minority unemployment in 1970 (Table 4-3). Also, it is widely held that minorities are substantially undercounted, perhaps by as much as 10 to 15 percent, by the census takers. Thus, gains are unlikely to be as large as the government income and employment figures would indicate.

Status of Minority Business Education

Studies show that technical and business education is closely related to successful small business development, yet minorities have been even more disadvantaged in the pursuit of education opportunities than in the income and employment areas.[26] In the area of formal business training, consider the following statistics. In the years since the inception of graduate business education in this country (1908), less than 600 minority group members received graduate business degrees through 1969. Of these, about 350 were graduates of the Atlanta University School of Business Administration (a predominately black university). In 1973, there were approximately 2,000 Ph.D. and D.B.A. candidates enrolled in U.S. schools of business, but less than 150 of these were minority group members.[27] There are today less than 150 minority persons holding doctorates in business or economics.[28] In 1969, of approximately 100,000 certified public accountants in the United States, only about 150 were black.[29] The data for Mexican–Americans and native Americans are even more discouraging.[30] Other statistics show that while 21.7 percent of all white males from 25 to 34 years old have completed four or more years of college, only 6.5 percent of black males in the same age bracket have done the same.[31] At the same time, 58.7 percent of blacks over 20 have not completed high school, compared with 36.4 percent of whites.[32]

Another voluntary survey undertaken by Educational Testing Services indicates that in the 1972-73 academic year, out of 67,000 students enrolled in full- and part-time M.B.A. programs, 4,252 or almost 7 percent are minority students. Certainly this is an improvement, but it still is not the kind of improvement that will provide parity of opportunity in business and management within the near future. Given present enrollment, about 12,000 would be required to reach parity, and untold additional thousands would be required to reach parity among graduate M.B.A.'s.

Psychological Reasons for Federal Involvement [33]

The above statistics detail the enormous economic and educational inequities that still exist for members of minority groups and give some insight into how they are perpetuated. They are the product of centuries of disregard, discrimination, and institutional racism. A major, long-term commitment of resources, energy, and imagination is required if the United States is to remedy this centuries-old injustice. Without a national effort, minority enterprise will likely experience gradual growth over the next several decades. However, it is increasingly apparent that a large-scale effort must be made to telescope the process of economic development. The nation cannot afford to wait, as the alternative is a continuation of the profound alienation of minority groups from our economic and social system, with unfortunate consequences for all Americans.

Throughout the nation's minority communities, there is a growing demand for sufficient economic independence to participate effectively in the system. Too often, a lack of access to the power structure breeds an atmosphere of frustration and anger. Bombarded hourly by television and other media displaying the wealth of our society, the disadvantaged, particularly the poor, cannot help but be aware of the discrepancy between their economic condition and that of the larger society. Blacks, American Indians, and Americans of Spanish-speaking ancestry are becoming increasingly determined to participate in the larger society through the exercise of their own economic, social, and political institutions.

The very existence of a large number of thriving minority entrepreneurs would boost the self-confidence of minority group members. Visible evidence of success would have a healthy psychological impact on the community and, unlike governmentally financed social welfare programs, the development of minority enterprise is one step toward a long-term solution to the problems of poverty and exclusion. Successful minority enterprise must largely be the product of minority ingenuity and effort, fostered by self-reliance, not dependence. It is, therefore, in the best interest of the nation to foster and accelerate the process of minority enterprise growth through involvement at the federal, state, and local levels.

Development of a Minority Capitalism Concept

In 1964, Gene Foley (SBA Administrator) initiated the "black capitalism" concept. His orientation grew out of a conviction that blacks do not want to integrate into the larger community. The ghetto is their sub-culture and they are familiar with it. Many minorities want to stay in their indigenous communities and develop them into viable economic and social units. As Foley states, the ghetto and barrio are "the world at which the upper classes wince in embarrassment, and which race leaders point to as proof that Negroes have been victimized. But for the masses of ghetto dwellers, this is a warm and familiar milieu, preferable to the sanitary coldness of middle-class neighborhoods."[34] Foley started the "six-by-six" program by which loans up to $6,000 were made to businessmen for six years with little or no collateral but with a special management program designed for the very small businessman. A non-profit corporation, called the Small Business Opportunities Corporation, was set up to oversee the program.[35] The management program of the corporation centered on day-to-day problems of running a business; counseling was provided by successful businessmen and, after the first year of operation, 98 loans were made to black businessmen without a single default.[36]

The program then became Title IV of the Equal Opportunity Act Amendments of 1966 and the loans became Equal Opportunity Loans (EOL), with a $25,000 limit, directly funded and administered by the Small Business Development Centers. However, under OEO the delinquency rate on loan repayment rose to 20 percent and threatened to climb higher.[37] The loans were eagerly sought by black entrepreneurs, but the program was not fully supported by the administration and the Congress.[38] Also, the program was unable to tap the resources of private financial organizations. In the first year, only six banks participated in Equal Opportunity Loans.[39]

In the summer of 1968, Howard J. Samuels, successor to Eugene Foley as administrator of the SBA, created Project Own, later to become Operation Mainstream in the Nixon Administration.[40] This project represented a major thrust in stimulating loans to minority businessmen, and the "black capitalism" concept was broadened to a concept of "minority capitalism" with the SBA being empowered to guarantee up to 90 percent of loans made by banks. Initially, Samuels aimed to increase the annual number of loans made to minority businessmen from 2,200 in 1968 to a rate of 20,000 by 1970.[41] In terms of money, he hoped that banks could expand loans to minority businessmen to ten times the then current level of $50 million.[42] Samuels also requested rules changes on approving loans which would emphasize the borrower's profit potential rather than his collateral.

At the same time, Samuels provided Project Own with teams of two or three SBA employees working in each of 70 selected cities in the United

States. These people worked with such local organizations as the Urban League and the National Business League to develop prospects for loans and to directly or indirectly provide management and technical assistance to selected loan recipients. A number of major changes, which became applicable to all SBA financial assistance programs, were made in SBA lending criteria under Project Own. These included relaxation of restrictions on "buyouts" (plans to change ownership of a going concern from one individual to another), equity participation for new businesses, and collateral requirements. Flexible repayment provisions were adopted and restrictions on loans for liquor stores and certain kinds of amusement places were eliminated. In addition, Samuels urged bankers to depart from their usual criteria for lending and to accept the notion of "compensatory capitalism," which implied accepting minority loans with higher risk than normal banking criteria would allow.[43]

Minority Economic Development and the Nixon Administration

The black capitalism program of Eugene Foley and Howard Samuels was greatly enlarged under the Nixon Administration, both within the SBA and more generally throughout the federal government; it also was expanded to include persons of Latin American, Mexican, and Indian ancestry. However, the expansion was accomplished largely by the use of existing agencies and procedures.

On March 5, 1969, two months after his inauguration, President Nixon issued an Executive Order that prescribed a series of steps for coordinating a national program for minority enterprises development. This Executive Order (#11458) established within the Department of Commerce an agency—the Office of Minority Business Enterprise (OMBE)—to develop and coordinate the federal government's program regarding minority enterprise.[44]

Federal spending in minority enterprise development increased from $212 million in fiscal year (FY) 1969 to more than $1.4 billion in FY 1973 (Tables 4-1 and 4-2). OMBE divides this spending into four categories: loans and loan guarantees, grants, procurement, and construction. SBA spending alone increased from a loan total of $107 million in FY 1969 to about $464 million in FY 1973 and a projected rate of more than $550 million for FY 1974. A summary of all federal agency spending for FY's 1969-73 is presented in Table 4-1. A number of these specific federal programs are briefly described below.

FEDERAL AGENCY PROGRAMS [45]

Small Business Administration (SBA)

Clearly the agency with the biggest involvement in minority enterprise, SBA, in fiscal 1971 spent more than one-half of the federal dollars allocated for assisting minority businesses. The SBA administers the following programs to assist minority small business (see Table 4-4):

Table 4-4. Small Business Administration Financial Assistance Activity (Dollars in Millions)

Fiscal Year	Loan Program	Total Loans Number	Approval Amount	Minority Loans Number	Approval Amount	Percentage Minority Number to Total Number	Percentage Number to Total Amount
1968	7A	9,460	$ 496.2	874	$ 21.7	9%	4%
	EOL	2,899	31.4	1,365	14.6	47	46
	DBL	327	44.8	29	1.3	9	3
	LDC	414	51.9	67	3.7	16	7
	(502)	13,100	$ 624.3	2,335	$ 41.3	18%	7%
1969	7A	9,483	547.9	1,460	58.3	15%	11%
	EOL	4,244	51.2	3,118	38.2	73	75
	DBL	283	33.5	20	1.3	7	4
	LDC	513	66.7	56	6.8	11	10
		14,523	$ 699.3	4,654	$104.6	32%	15%
1970	7A	8,719	$ 528.3	1,629	$ 84.4	19%	16%
	EOL	5,539	72.6	4,505	60.6	81	83
	DBL	338	41.5	23	2.9	7	7
	LDC	506	67.1	105	12.5	21	19
		15,102	$ 709.6	6,262	$160.4	41%	23%
1971	7A	13,754	933.9	2,123	$121.5	15.4 %	13.0 %
	EOL	6,789	92.8	5,451	75.7	80.0	81.6
	DBL	386	40.9	31	1.6	8.0	3.9
	LDC	561	60.9	171	14.9	30.4	24.4
		21,490	$1,128.5	7,776	$213.7	36.1 %	18.9 %
1972	7A	$19,881	$1,366.6	3,099	$165.4	15%	12%
	EOL	7,167	92.6	5,791	74.0	81	80
	DBL	336	35.3	36	2.4	–	–
	LDC	641	81.3	140	16.4	22	20
		$28,028	$1,575.8	9,016	$258.2	32%	16%
1973	7A	25,219	$1,926.5	3,285	200.9		20%
	EOL	7,692	148.5	5,557	110.0		75
	DBL	329	41.9	29	2.5		–
	LDC	708	79.2	203	20.5		16
		$33,948	$2,194.2	4,074	334.0		21%

Source: Data provided by SBA 1973.

1. Regular Business Loans—Section 7(a);
2. Displaced Business Loans;
3. Local Development Company 502 Loans;
4. Equal Opportunity Loans (EOL);
5. Federal Procurement Contract Assistance—Section 8(a).

SBA also encourages equity investments in minority business through the Minority Enterprise Small Business Investment Corporations (MESBIC). Only marginal changes have been made in the enabling legislation in these financial programs. The adaptation to a minority focus came about largely as the result of Executive Office direction.

SBA Regular Business Loans. The SBA Regular Business Loan Program is established by Section 7(a) of the SBA Act of 1953, as amended (1958). This section allows SBA to guarantee up to 90 percent or $350,000 (whichever is smaller) of a bank loan to a small business enterprise. Alternatively, if the loan cannot be obtained entirely from a private lender and if an SBA-guaranteed loan is not available, SBA may advance up to $150,000 on an immediate participation basis with a bank. Finally, if neither of the above alternatives is available, SBA is authorized to make a direct loan up to $100,000.

Displaced Business Loans (DBL). The Displaced Business Loan Program was instituted to reimburse small businesses that suffer an economic loss as a result of construction by or with federal funding. This economic disaster program is applicable to minority and other small businesses that are either physically displaced or economically disadvantaged as a result of urban renewal and related government efforts to reclaim and renovate inner-city areas.

This program provides long-term loans or guarantees for up to ten years, with no dollar limit. SBA does impose limits, however, on the upgrading or expansion of businesses with DBL funds.

Local Development Company 502 Loans. LDC/502 Loans are awarded to Local Development Companies, chartered for profit or not-for-profit, so that these companies can provide long-term financing to small businesses in their areas. Loans to LDC's may not be utilized for working capital or for refinancing purposes.

Economic Opportunity Loans (EOL). The Economic Opportunity Loan Program (EOL) provides financial assistance, advisory services, and counseling to qualified members of minorities with low incomes. Qualified minorities include those people who, because of race, color, religion, or ethnic origin, have been denied the chance to obtain adequate business financing through normal channels.

The program, which was established by the 1966 amendment to the Economic Opportunity Act of 1964, provides for loans of up to $25,000 with up to fifteen-year repayment periods to potential or existing businesses. The Act was amended in 1972 to allow a $50,000 maximum. The loans may be provided directly by SBA, or the agency may participate in or guarantee EOL loans with commercial banking institutions. In addition to financial assistance, the EOL program provides some funds for professional management and technical assistance upon request of the loanee. However, these funds have been minimal and recently (1973) this function was transferred to OMBE.

Federal Procurement Assistance—Section 8(a).   Under Section 8(a) of the SBA Act, SBA is empowered to contract with federal procurement agencies for supplies and services. SBA then subcontracts with a small business firm to furnish goods and/or services. This provision permits SBA to channel government purchases to small firms that might otherwise not be able to compete successfully with larger firms.

Minority Enterprise Small Business Investment Companies (MESBIC)

A specialized form of Small Business Investment Company (SBIC), authorized by the Small Business Investment Act of 1958, was devised to aid in financing minority businesses. A MESBIC is a private investment corporation, like an SBIC, that specializes in providing long-term venture capital. But, unlike an SBIC, a MESBIC may provide management assistance to its clients, minority businesses.[46] A MESBIC is an SBIC with the following important differences:

1. The MESBIC investments are made solely in businesses which are at least 51 percent minority-owned.
2. The MESBIC has the support of a strong "sponsor"—that is, some organization or group that can directly or indirectly provide the necessary capital, operating funds, and management assistance to the MESBIC and its portfolio companies.
3. A MESBIC can be licensed with a minimum capital of $150,000 but SBA imposes the restriction that annual operating expenses in excess of $10–12,000 cannot be drawn from this minimum capital. Some other arrangement must be made to cover the balance of costs, usually involving the assistance of the "sponsor."

As with regular SBIC's, a MESBIC is formed when private investors (the "sponsors") put up the minimum required capital, incorporate as an investment company, and obtain a license to operate from the Small Business Administration. After the MESBIC is in operation, it is eligible to borrow $2 from the SBA for every $1 of private capital, from a minimum of $300,000 to a maximum of $20 million (3:1 matching for all investments over $500,000). The loans are in the form of ten to fifteen-year subordinated debentures at an interest rate equal to the federal government's cost of money for similar securities. These funds, together with the equity investment in the MESBIC, are for "seed capital" investment in minority businesses, either in the form of subordinated long-term loans (five to twenty years) or equity. The MESBIC is not allowed to take a controlling interest in the ventures it finances. Most MESBIC investments have been in the form of subordinated long-term debentures and not as equity investments, thereby increasing the debt/equity ratio of their client minority entrepreneurs.

Office of Minority Business Enterprise (OMBE)

OMBE, under the Department of Commerce, is the coordinating agency for all minority enterprise programs, nationwide. It also has principal responsibility for providing technical assistance to existing minority entrepreneurs through a large number of local Business Development Organizations (LBDOs) located in almost 100 urban and rural areas.

As the result of a recent Department of Commerce Task Force evaluation of the OMBE program, there was a complete reorganization and decentralization of the agency with the following structural changes and functional emphases: [47]

1. Seventy percent of the OMBE staff money was allocated to establish six fully-staffed regional offices in New York, Washington, D.C., Atlanta, Chicago, Dallas, and San Francisco. The Regional Directors of these offices report directly to the Director of OMBE in the Washington, D.C. Headquarters Office. Each Regional Director is assisted by a Deputy Regional Director and a technical support staff of five highly trained specialists—one for each of the major OMBE program areas: education and training, finance, government and private procurement, and construction contracting. In addition to the six regional offices, there are district offices in ten or more additional cities that have field offices involved in the day-to-day monitoring and evaluation of individual contracts. These Field Officers report to the Regional Director and receive specialized supportive services from the technical specialists mentioned above. This emphasis on close contract supervision reflects the fact that the bulk of the OMBE budget is invested through more than 300 contractor and grantee OMBE–funded organizations. Also, under the former, centralized structure it was felt that there were serious deficiencies as a result of the great physical distance between the OMBE staff and the contractors.

The Washington, D.C., Headquarters Office has been reorganized into two divisions: a) the National Programs Division, staffed with government and corporate executives who develop, negotiate, and coordinate minority business opportunity resources with other federal agencies and with private industry; and b) the Administration and Field Coordination Division, staffed with persons skilled in administrative functions such as program analysis, budget and financial management analysis, and automated information. This Division develops the policy and procedural guidelines to coordinate the field effort and assist the regional offices.

The reorganization and decentralization of OMBE is expected to improve direct services to the minority entrepreneur, tailor the program to meet unique and specialized regional and local conditions, lead to greater resource development in each region, improve coordination and evaluation of programs through frequent on-site visits, increase utilization of management and technical assistance, and provide more accurate data upon which to base future decisions through on-site verification of contractor reports.

2. A strong effort is being made to train business development staffs in OMBE-funded organizations in pre-locational marketing analysis to avoid arranging loans for businesses which have few realistic prospects of success.

3. OMBE, in order to maximize minority business success, is attempting to match high leverage opportunities with very capable minority entrepreneurs and sufficient capital. In addition, OMBE is making efforts to develop particularly high leverage opportunities.[48]

4. OMBE attempts to promote greater coordination betweeen and development of federal and private resources so that specific minority businesses not only can produce goods and services, but can develop the capacity to market them in the private sector and to the government on a bid basis.

5. In June 1972 OMBE initiated its Performance Management System to evaluate the performance of its funded organizations and identify the least productive of them. It will continue to utilize this system in order to direct its funding toward the most promising ventures. However, little hard data has yet been generated to indicate the value of this system.

Economic Development Administration (EDA)

The EDA of the Department of Commerce has as its primary goal the economic development of geographical areas in which there is substantial and persistent unemployment or underemployment. To accomplish this goal, its programs are focused on improvement of the economic potential of an area so that it will be able to attract additional economic activity. A significant portion of EDA's assistance is spent to improve a blighted area's infrastructure, such as public facilities. In addition, EDA awards large, low-interest, long-term loans to major businesses wishing to locate in the designated areas. These businesses are expected to generate significant employment to alleviate some of the unemployment in the area. These loans usually are awarded to larger businesses; the average amount of an EDA loan is $1 million. The EDA program also includes public works grants and loans, business loans for industrial and commercial facilities, guarantees for private working capital loans, and technical planning and research assistance for areas designated as redevelopment areas by the Assistant Secretary of Commerce.

The Nixon Administration attempted to dismantle EDA. So far, Congress has not agreed, but the future of the organization is in doubt.

Office of Economic Opportunity (OEO)

OEO was created in the Executive Office of the President under the Economic Opportunity Act of 1964. The Act, as amended in 1966 and 1967, authorizes OEO to become involved in financing programs of sufficient size to have an impact on the economies of both urban and rural communities. These programs may be of the following types:

1. Economic and business development programs, including programs that provide financial and other incentives to business to locate where they provide employment opportunities for underprivileged persons; and programs for small businesses located in or owned by residents of such areas;
2. Community development activities that create new training and employment opportunities and that contribute to an improved living environment; and
3. Manpower training programs, for unemployed or low-income persons, that support and complement economic, business, and community development programs.

In the period 1964 to 1966, the major thrust in economic development was in the development of job training and placement programs. Beginning in 1966, OEO began in a small way (under $2 million) to develop an economic development program based primarily on the sponsorship of community development corporations (CDCs). These CDCs were to engage in enterprise development programs, both by way of direct ownership and by way of investment.

The CDC program was placed under the direction of the Economic Development Division (EDD). However, funding for EDD was never more than a small fraction of that provided for manpower development programs (about 5 percent). Typically, OEO has made a multi-year grant (two to three years) to the private not-for-profit CDC. This grant may then be utilized by the CDC to provide equity capital, loans, loan guarantees and other developmental assistance to minority entrepreneurs who live in or operate in the local community, or for direct ownership by the CDC.[49]

The other important OEO program in the area of minority enterprise development is sponsorship of the Opportunity Funding Corporation (OFC), which was initiated by EDD in June 1970 as discussed in Chapter 5.

Evolution of the Community Development Concept

Parallel to the development of a minority capitalism concept in the federal government was a movement that originated in the Economic Development Division of OEO. This movement, headed by the then director of EDD, Geoffrey Faux, aimed at establishing CDCs in ghetto areas of large urban centers in the country. These corporations, using Title ID (Amendment in 1966 to OEO Act) to provide funds for areas of substantial poverty designated as "Special Impact funds," have implemented economic development programs in these depressed areas.

The Special Impact Program authorized by Title ID of the Economic Opportunity Act has been primarily used to support CDCs. It was specifically written into the Act in 1966 to support an economic development project in the Bedford–Stuyvesant section of Brooklyn (Bedford–Stuyvesant Restoration Corporation). The late Senator Robert F. Kennedy, as well as Senator Jacob Javits were principal movers behind the creation of the Restoration Corporation and the Development and Services Corporation, two separate corporations set up to run the Bedford–Stuyvesant program. These corporations were an alliance of businessmen and ghetto residents designed to minimize the influence of the city and anti-poverty federal bureaucracies. To finance the program, Kennedy and Javits introduced an amendment to Title I of the Economic Opportunity Act that authorized Special Impact Programs for urban areas with high concentrations of low-income residents. The language of Title ID is imprecise; the details of the program had not been completely worked out prior to the passage of the Amendment.[50] It was the intent of the program that decisions should be made at the local level and that the business community alliance should be as free as possible to respond to needs and opportunities. For fiscal 1967, $25 million was appropriated, with $6.9 million going to Bedofrd–Stuyvesant. The remainder was scattered into various projects under the Labor Department's Concentrated Employment Program (CEP).[51]

The politics became intense at this point. After a great deal of bureaucratic maneuvering, Title ID (Special Impact) funds were scattered to four agencies: the Departments of Labor, Commerce, Agriculture, and OEO, with the latter getting $1.6 million,[52] the smallest part of the total.

In 1967, the Green Amendment to the OEO Act was passed. A major intent of the amendment was to placate the southern Democrats (who have historically resented federal interference in local politics) and to solidify the support of the big-city Democratic mayors (e.g., Mayor Richard J. Daley of Chicago); there had been a noticeable conflict between city hall and the local anti-poverty groups in most machine-dominated cities. It was also an attempt to blunt the efforts of the Republicans who wanted to dismember or "spin off" OEO into existing agencies. By giving the illusion of citizen control, the Republican alternatives could be made less appealing. Representative Carl D. Perkins (D.-Kentucky), chairman of the Education and Labor Committee, conceded that committee acceptance of the Green Amendment was "dictated by political necessity to insure the continuation of the poverty program."[53] Many Republicans and some liberal Democrats characterized the amendment as an extension of city hall domination or the "bosses and boll weevil" amendment.

However, they were unable to form a coalition strong enough to defeat it on the House floor.

This event signaled the crumbling of the anti-poverty constituency's power over the bureaucracy. It was widely held in minority community circles that *flexibility* at the community level was required for effective CDC operation; however, this hardening of the bureaucracy's demands for accountability came at the expense of the CDC's freedom of operation. This laying on of bureaucratic red tape and the resultant conflicts over community control effectively stalled both project planning and implementation.

The Setting for the Initiation of OFC

President Nixon's Republican Administration, coming to office in 1968, was not too sympathetic to OEO in general and to the CDCs in particular. In 1969, Mr. Nixon appointed Donald Rumsfeld, a former Chicago North Shore congressman, to head OEO. Rumsfeld showed early in his tenure that he wanted each of the local CDCs to be held directly accountable to OEO. He felt that making grants without tight controls was irresponsible:

> What happens if ten years from now the Black Panthers are chosen by the stockholders to *run* one of these CDCs? How are you going to prevent that?[54]

The situation then was the following:

1. Rumsfeld, a Republican, wanted to push a capitalist-oriented economic development program that embodied Mr. Nixon's values.
2. Title ID funds were the only ones readily available because of the amendment's loose wording.
3. Rumsfeld was not enthusiastic about the CDC concept to begin with.
4. No experimental device existed for the testing of Theodore Cross' theory of black capitalism (which embodied the value structure of the administration).

It was in this environment that OFC was created to test a variety of financial incentives outlined in Theodore Cross' book *Black Capitalism* (New York: Atheneum, 1969). Rumsfeld wanted a quasi-public corporation, semi-independent from OEO, run by business executives (so that the federal bureaucracy could be side-stepped), and designed to be an experimental/demonstration program.

Before proceeding with the case study, let us summarize how OFC fits into this network of federal programs and what its role is (or should be). Out of a combined federal effort of almost $3.4 billion since FY 1969, OFC's

$8.1 million in funding looks meager indeed. Yet, OFC is unique among these federal programs in that its charter is to *experiment* with the use of *indirect* or *secondary* financing techniques designed, through the *use of financial leverage,* in order to induce the flow of private section capital into economically depressed areas.

"Fannie Mae" and "Ginny Mae" (in the housing finance area) with their secondary market activities are analogous to the OFC concept. OFC was intended to be an experimentation/demonstration program whose ultimate goal was to transfer its technology to other government agencies that have the resources and clout really to put them to use.

There are some questions that do need to be asked about OFC. In the first place, has OFC experimented in the right areas? The biggest need for minority businessmen is for venture capital or equity money, not for loans; yet much of the OFC effort has been directed to making more debt capital available. Is OFC then serving a critical need? Secondly, is it realistic to assume that OFC's technology can be effectively transferred to other governmental agencies? There is some indication in the following case study that OFC wants to expand into a national minority funding corporation with the financial clout to implement its proven programs. What will be the political disposition of this ultimate conflict area? These and other related questions should be kept in mind as the case study of OFC's politics of evaluation proceeds.

One final point relates to the environment in which OFC is to be evaluated. OFC operates in a social-economic-political environment that is constantly changing and over which OFC has little or no control. This means that a field evaluation research of OFC's programs will have to contend with changes in variables—quite possibly stronger than the experimental variable(s)— over which the evaluator has no direct or indirect control. The evaluators of OFC's programs have opted for a qualitative, process-oriented design, perhaps for this reason. There are some interesting political ramifications of this dilemma that are explored in the next chapter, the case study of OFC's politics of evaluation experience.

NOTES

1. U.S. Constitution, Article I, Section 8 (3).
2. National League of Cities, *Federal Budget and the Cities: A Review of the President's 1974 Budget in the Light of Urban Needs and National Priorities* (Washington, D.C.: National League of Cities, February 1973) and *Budget of the United States, 1973 and 1974.* Sponsorship of law enforcement grants has gone from $59 million in FY 1969 to a projected $891 million in FY 1974, or an increase of almost 1500 percent in 5 years.

3. *Steele vs. Louisville and Nashville Railroad*, 323 U.S. 192 (1944).

4. See report of the National League of Cities, *Federal Budget and the Cities*.

5. Michael Sovern, *Legal Restraints on Racial Discrimination in Employment* (New York: Twentieth Century Fund, 1966), p. 5.

6. Ibid., pp. 40–53.

7. Richard Bardolph (ed.), *The Civil Rights Record: Black Americans and the Law* (New York: Thomas Y. Crowell Co., 1970), p. 17.

8. Ibid., p. 534.

9. Ibid.

10. Ibid., p. 535.

11. Richard Nathan, *Jobs and Civil Rights* (Washington, D.C.: U.S. Commission on Civil Rights, April 1969), p. 14.

12. Ibid., p. 18.

13. Civil Rights Act of 1964 as Amended.

14. Ibid., sec. 706.

15. Executive Order No. 11246, signed by Lyndon B. Johnson, September 24, 1965 (Section 202-1).

16. See generally Neil Chamberlain and Donald Cullen, *The Labor Sector* (New York: McGraw-Hill, 1971), Chapters 21 to 25 for a discussion of government intervention in the labor market to ensure greater social protection for workers.

17. "JOBS Program Gets Poor Marks," *Business and Society* (September 8, 1970). See also Robert Yancy, Stewart Krawil and John Rahiya, "The National Alliance of Businessmen: Its Purposes, Interaction and Results," in Samuel Doctors (ed.), *Whatever Happened to Minority Economic Development,* (Chicago: Dryden Press, 1974), pp. 74–9.

18. U.S. Department of Commerce, Bureau of the Census, *Minority Owned Businesses: 1969* (Washington, D.C.: U.S. Government Printing Office, November 1971, pp. 1–2. The new census of minority businesses (for 1972) is complete only for black-owned businesses. It shows a 32 percent increase in sales and a 7 percent increase in number of businesses. U.S. Department of Commerce, Bureau of the Census, *1972 Survey of Minority-Owned Businesses - Black* (Washington, D.C.: Bureau of the Census, November 1974), pp. 14–15. During this same three-year period (1969 to 1972), non-minority business sales grew by more than 20 percent.

19. Ibid.

20. Ibid.

21. The sales figure for Motown Industries is from "The Nation's 100 Top Black Businesses," *Black Enterprise* (June 1973), p. 37; the sales figure for Varian Associates is from *Fortune 500* (May 1973), p. 240.

22. The 0.3 percent figure was supplied by OMBE in 1972 and the $859 billion is from *Statistical Abstract of the U.S. 1972,* 93rd ed. (Washington, D.C.: U.S. Government Printing Office, 1972), pp. 438, 477.

23. Ibid.

24. James H. Weaver, "Economic Causes of Social Unrest," unpublished paper, American University, Economics Department, 1972.
25. Ibid.; also various Census Bureau special studies on minority social and economic status.
26. Samuel Doctors and Michael Belletire, "Education and Training: The Missing Ingredient in Minority Capitalism," *Journal of Small Business Management* (Fall 1973), pp. 11–16. See also Edward Denison, *The Sources of Economic Growth in the United States and the Alternatives Before Us* (New York: Committee for Economic Development, 1962); Robert Solow, "Technical Change and the Aggregate Productions Function," *Review of Economics and Statistics* 39, No. 3 (August 1957), pp. 312–20; Edward Roberts, "Technical Entrepreneurship" in Donald Marquis and William Gruber (eds.), *Factors in Technology Transfer* (Cambridge, Mass.: the M.I.T. Press, 1969), pp. 219–37. See also Samuel Doctors and Anthony Akel, "Federal R & D Expenditures and Industrial Productivity," *Business Perspectives* (Summer 1973).
27. American Assembly of Collegiate Schools of Business, "Enrollment of Minority Doctoral Students by Institution and Program" (October 1973). It is believed that these figures may be somewhat inflated.
28. HEW Task Force on Minority Business Education and Training Preliminary Report, January 1973.
29. Bert Mitchell, "The Black Minority in the C.P.A. Profession," *The Journal of Accountancy* (October 1969), pp. 41–48.
30. See U.S. Senate Committee on Labor and Public Welfare, *Indian Education: A National Tragedy—A National Challenge* (Washington, D.C.: U.S. Government Printing Office, 1969), p. 80; and Leo Grebler et al., *The Mexican-American People* (New York: The Free Press, 1970), p. 216.
31. U.S. Department of Commerce, Current Population Reports, *The Social and Economic Status of the Black Population in the United States* (Washington, D.C.: U.S. Government Printing Office, July 1972), p. 84.
32. Department of Commerce, Current Population Reports, *Educational Attainment, March 1972* (Washington, D.C.: U.S. Government Printing Office, 1973), p. 7.
33. Much of the material in the following section is paraphrased from The President's Advisory Council on Minority Business Enterprise, *Minority Enterprise and Expanded Ownership: Blueprint for the Seventies* (Washington, D.C.: U.S. Government Printing Office, June 1971), pp. 5–7.
34. Eugene Foley, *The Achieving Ghetto* (Washington, D.C.: The Washington National Press, 1968), p. 21.
35. Ibid., p. 140.
36. James M. Hund, *Black Entrepreneurship* (Belmont, Calif.: Wadsworth Publishing Co., 1970), p. 43.
37. Robert McKersie, "Vitalize Black Enterprise," *Harvard Business Review* 46, No. 5 (September–October 1968), p. 92.

38. Hund, *Black Entrepreneurship.*
39. Sar Levitan *et al., Economic Opporunity in the Ghetto: The Partnership of Government and Business* (Baltimore: The Johns Hopkins Press, 1970), p. 9.
40. Hund, *Black Entrepreneurship,* p. 47.
41. Actual figures for FY 1970 were a total of 6,262 loans and loan guarantees to minority entrepreneurs for a total dollar volume of $160.4 million or about 15 percent of all SBA loans and loan guarantees. See U.S. Department of Commerce, OMBE, *Report to the President on Minority Business Enterprise* (Washington, D.C.: OMBE, June 30, 1970), p. III–13.
42. Hund, *Black Entrepreneurship,* p. 48.
43. See Howard Samuels, "Compensatory Capitalism," in William F. Haddad and G. Douglas Pugh (eds.), *Black Economic Development* (Englewood Cliffs, N.J.: Prentice-Hall, 1969), pp. 60–73, for a full discussion of this concept.
44. "Statement by the President on Minority Enterprise," *Public Papers of the President of the U.S.* (Washington, D.C.: Office of the Federal Register, National Archives and Records Service, March 5, 1970).
45. See, generally, U.S. Department of Commerce, OMBE, *Special Catalog of Federal Programs Assisting Minority Enterprise* (Washington, D.C.: U.S. G.P.O., Summer 1971), for a description of federal minority enterprise programs.
46. U.S. Department of Commerce, Office of Minority Business Enterprise, *MESBICs and Minority Enterprise* (Washington, D.C.: U.S. Government Printing Office, December 1970), p. 5.
47. Material provided by OMBE, September 1973.
48. This new OMBE emphasis follows the recommendation of PACMBE, *Minority Enterprise and Expanded Ownership,* pp. 1, 21, and 35–36. This new high growth emphasis may represent a significant shift in OMBE policy.
49. See Twentieth Century Fund, *CDC's: New Hope for the Inner City* (New York: Twentieth Century Fund, 1971) for a detailed description of CDC programs.
50. Geoffrey Faux, "Politics and Bureaucracy in Community-Controlled Economic Development," *Law and Contemporary Problems* (Spring 1971) p. 282. Also see more generally, John Donovan, *The Politics of Poverty* (New York: Pegasus, 1967).
51. Ibid.
52. Ibid., p. 283.
53. See *Congress and the Nation: A Review of Government and Politics,* Vol. II, 1965–68 (Washington, D.C.: Congressional Quarterly Service, 1969), p. 135.
54. Faux, "Politics and Bureaucracy," p. 292.

Chapter Five

The Politics of Evaluation Research at the Opportunity Funding Corporation (OFC)

This chapter reports an empirical investigation of the OFC experience concerning the evaluation of its effectiveness vis-a-vis its goals. The intent is to accurately recreate, through personal interviews and selected secondary sources, the power and influence processes that affected decision-making at OFC with regard to evaluation. This chronology of events covers the period November, 1969 (the initial articulation of the OFC concept) to July, 1972 (after the publication of the first interim report on the evaluation of the Surety Bonding Program).

As mentioned in Chapter Three, within a government agency evaluation is a political activity. It is in this context that this empirical study is presented.

The epilogue presented after Chapter Six briefly relates and analyzes the operation of OFC from July 1972 to March 1974. This epilogue also includes an analysis of the conclusions described in Chapter Six in light of the subsequent twenty months of OFC operations.

It is appropriate at this time to refocus attention on the methodology to be utilized in this analysis. As was stated in Chapter One, a process research approach is used. This qualitive research orientation uses the historical case study method. The method is concerned with the development of events through time. The intent is to use a single case as a basis of support or refutation of an existing body of theory and to generate new hypotheses relevant to that theory.[1]

The data analysis proceeds through three levels of generalization. First, the material in this chapter presents a description of what happened at OFC over time with regard to evaluation by describing the actual actors and events. This data is then used in Chapter Six to focus attention on the validity of the theoretical material presented in Chapter Three. Finally, the analysis in Chapter Six proceeds to a higher level of abstraction, wherein experience gained in the OFC case analysis is used to suggest structural and/or behavioral changes that might facilitate the more advantageous use of evaluation research in the social agency setting.

There are some final points that should be reviewed prior to beginning the empirical investigation. It should be emphasized that both Attribution Theory and Sociometric Analysis are not used in their classic analytical modes. Rather, they are adapted for use in this particular analysis as practical tools for visualizing and thinking about what is important about the power and influence relationships between the several major actors in the OFC affair. Also, two distinct types of interview data are used in the case study and their differences will be noted in the text. Most of the interview data used in the case study were collected within the period February to July 1972.* These data are used to develop a chronology of the events in OFC's politics of evaluation. A second set of data was then collected. A select group of influential actors not interviewed during the February to July 1972 phase were asked to review the case study as constructed on the basis of the data from those respondents interviewed in the first phase. This technique has a two-fold purpose: (1) to cross-verify the construction of the OFC case, hopefully to catch any factual errors that might have occurred, and (2) perhaps more importantly, to get further commentary on critical perceptions in the case. Areas on which the actors felt inclined to comment were likely to be those areas that were particularly relevant to them, and will be duly noted in the text. Several interviews were conducted during the late summer of 1973 to bring this case study up to date on OFC operations, and this data is included in the Epilogue. Finally, it must be remembered that the quotes are not to be considered "facts" in the analysis; rather, they represent only the perceptions of a particular actor at a particular time. Conflicts in perception over certain points will be amplified in the text. It is not the position of these researchers to take a stand on fact vs. rationalization but merely to recognize that both (plus selectively distorted memory) probably influence the data.

A HISTORICAL OVERVIEW OF OFC

In November 1969, Donald Rumsfeld (then director of the Office of Economic Opportunity) received a copy of Theodore Cross' *Black Capitalism* and, upon reading it, became intrigued with the idea of implementing at OEO, an experimental/demonstration program based on the book.

The OFC model or program that grew out of Cross' book was designed, according to Cross' theory, to test various financial incentives (e.g., loan guarantees, interest subsidies, rediscounting of SBA paper) to see which

---

*Cross returned to his business interests after OFC was incorporated in late June of 1970 and took no active role in the actual operation of the Corporation.

combinations of them could most effectively leverage private money into the creation of a capital base in a ghetto environment. This OFC model represents an attempt to use existing financial technology (which has been aiding the white-dominated corporate elite for years) for the purpose of building capital attraction and retention mechanisms in the ghettos, barrios, and reservations of the country. The purpose was to reverse the traditional flow of capital out of the ghetto. Investment within the ghetto has traditionally been considered a poor business risk because of the poor capital base, high crime rate, low average income, high insurance rates, few support institutions, and general economic malaise.

The substance of OFC's uniqueness in comparison with existing federal programs is its use of financial leverage through secondary or indirect financing techniques. Through its various programs, OFC seeks to employ its funds so as to multiply the financial resources flowing into projects and business ventures that can benefit low-income communities. To achieve this financial leverage, OFC makes use of indirect financing grants, straight investments, and loans. In most instances, OFC's indirect financing provides the "missing link" for a venture—the impetus to convince a private capital or credit source to commit funds that in turn may tie together a complex package of investments, loans, and grants to finance an economic development project.

Three basic techniques that OFC can employ to gain financial leverage are:

1. Guaranties;
2. Secondary market activities;
3. Incentive payments.

Each of these techniques will be explored further when the separate programs are discussed. It must be remembered from Chapter One that a basic assumption underlying the use of these techniques is that, because investors perceive the risks of investing in the ghetto and other disadvantaged communities as being higher than normal, they may be persuaded to invest in them only if they are offered some degree of downside protection or, alternatively, added earnings potential.[2]

To return to the chronology of the case analysis, Rumsfeld called in Ted Cross, a wealthy, white Wall Street lawyer from New York to work part-time as a special consultant to OEO and to design an OEO-funded program that would effectively test his theory in a ghetto context. In January 1970 Cross, Victor Sparrow (a young, black White House fellow who was assigned to work with Cross by Rumsfeld), and Paul London (a young white urban affairs specialist from the American Management Association) began the initial design of the program. Cross was also given two full-time OEO secretaries. Cross spent the better part of six months in Washington with Sparrow, while

Paul London worked between New York and Washington, conducting support research for the project.* In addition, Professor Samuel I. Doctors was hired as a part-time consultant to OEO; Doctors helped Cross with some of the technical aspects of the design. Doctors was Cross' advisor with regard to the political problems with the embryonic OEO, although this authority was questioned by OEO workers. Doctors was consulted frequently by Cross for advice on such problems as strategic planning, potential funding sources, method of involving the hostile OEO people and militant blacks in the OFC project, and developing congressional contacts.

In formulating the design, Cross interviewed scores of white and minority business people, financial leaders, government officials and academicians. However, no minority community representatives were included in the planning and this led to "Project X" (as the Cross group was named) being hailed as another "phony white-run outfit."[3] Minority leaders were approached by Cross' group, but they would not be co-opted into participation in a program that they felt was a threat to their own community development funding.

The lack of minority input coupled with the project's secrecy created many public relations problems for Cross and his group. Project X ran into substantial political opposition at the outset. The complete secrecy of the project alienated the community development people at OEO who suspected that the money used to finance what was to become OFC would come from the Community Development Corporation (CDC) Title ID funds. Prior to this time, Title ID funds were used only for the CDCs. According to Cross and Don Lowitz, general counsel for OEO, the money used for OFC funding came from research and development funds, not CDC Title ID funds.

The initial OFC grant came from two OEO funds—three and a half million dollars of the $7.4 million originally provided to OFC came from R & D funds, the balance came from Title ID funds. (An additional $0.7 million was provided for staff salaries in 1972 for an eighteen month period.)

The CDC opposition was an effective lobby, and "Project X" succeeded in arousing its ire. The following statement of Devra Bloom, Ted Cross' secretary, illuminates the problem:

> The tough part was selling the CDCs on the program. They were very hostile to the program for several reasons. First, it was capitalism and profit-oriented and CDC people see this sometimes as the root of our society's problems. Secondly, they knew that the money was going to come out of their pot. Third, they resented the secrecy involved in the project. . . . Before OFC, everything in the EDD (Economic Development Division of OEO) budget was to go to CDCs; now, they had to share what they considered to be

*A complete list of interviews is provided in a separate section of the Bibliography.

limited funds with an agency whose main principles they did not like. In my opinion, the Administration wanted a "gimmick," a new program that strongly reflected Richard Nixon's values. So OFC's creation was inevitable. Since they were stuck with OFC, the CDCs wanted to insure that dollars put into ghetto banks by OFC would be available to the local CDCs. I think something has been worked out in that area.

Paul London agreed with this assessment:

> There was substantial opposition to the OFC concept . . . because OFC threatened to sap OEO Title ID funds for its operations which had formerly been used only by the CDCs. OFC had powerful enemies from the outset. The project, called "Project X" for its secrecy, was not even discussed with Geoffrey Faux, then the head of EDD. Faux is a leading CDC supporter . . . and the CDCs had a lot of support from vocal blacks. CDC allies were savvy in the political process, and had friends on both Gaylord Nelson's and Jacob Javits' committee. Ted (Cross) learned his political lessons the hard way—make friends with Javits and Nelson.

There is evidence to indicate that even some OEO officials were surprised at the intensity of the CDC opposition to OFC. As Donald Lowitz opined:

> My recollection is that, after the congressional meetings, discussions were held with the CDC groups and other groups within the poor community. We were surprised by the vocal opposition from the CDCs. We never viewed OFC as being a competitor to the CDC program and saw it as a possible aid to CDCs. Therefore, we were unprepared for the hostility that resulted.

To this end, Cross issued a memorandum which stated:

> There should be an early and important thrust toward building support with appropriate federal, state, and local officials, particularly with congressional committees who must pass on OFC funding and substantive programs. Not only must senators and congressmen interested in this area be educated, but *more important* key congressional committee staff personnel must be informed about OFC. Information is a key element to success in Congress; use knowledge about the potential of OFC for minority economic development as a vehicle for continuing contact with key staff and their congressional committee members (with a special interest in this area).

Funding, then, was one basis of the CDC/OFC conflict. It was assumed that OFC funding would necessarily come from the $30 to $35 million CDC Title ID funds. Powerful congressional leaders came to the CDC's defense. "I am concerned that the modest funding available under Title ID be used exclusively to aid community-based economic development projects as intended by Congress," Sen. Gaylord Nelson wrote to Donald Rumsfeld. A preliminary organization chart was "leaked" to Jack Anderson of *The Washington Post* in an effort to discredit Rumsfeld and the OFC concept. Yet, at that time, the ID funds (and the R & D funds) were apparently the only practicably obtainable source of stable funding available to OFC. Dick Cheney, aide to Donald Rumsfeld, noted:

> The biggest problem was how to fund it (OFC). OEO has enormous budget problems. It is very difficult to get money out of Congress; as a result, you will find many federal agencies spending vast amounts of excess money right before July 1 (the end of the fiscal year) so that they can justify next year's appropriations. Because of this, our funding goal for OFC was to provide stability for the organization. We wanted to insulate the program from normal tugs and pulls that OEO grantees run into. OFC would have to enter into long-term commitments with its programs, so stability is a must. We think the $7.4 million authorized is a good start in that direction.

By July 1970, this conflict had started to die down. It became evident to the CDC supporters that, with such a strong backer as Rumsfeld, OFC was going to be created. The CDCs then decided to change their strategy; they stopped trying to impede OFC's creation. Instead, they tried to minimize the ID funds granted to OFC.

The original "asking price" of $20 to $25 million for the initiation of OFC was pegged sufficiently high to allow for negotiations with the powerful CDC group so that they could "win" a reduced funding level for OFC. However, there is some evidence to indicate that Rumsfeld had promised Cross a budget of $20 million. Doctors had been asked by Cross to make up an organizational chart based on the $20 million figure.

Cross and the "Project X" people did take actions to placate both the militant CDC people and other minority community leaders. Cross issued the following strategic statement:

> There is a need to inform CDCs and other community people as to the importance of OFC to them. The mere fact that OFC will obviously benefit these groups, long-term, is not enough. Someone must be assigned to provide a continuing liaison function with community people. The people represent a most important part of the OFC constituency.

Meetings were held to iron out differences and minimize opposition to OFC.

THE THEORETICAL BASE OF OFC: CROSS' THEORY OF BLACK CAPITALISM

In his *Black Capitalism,* Cross argues that there will never be enough money to fund minority economic development entirely from federal sources. Ways must be found to leverage the enormous talent and capital of the private sector to have a real impact on the problems of the disadvantaged in this country. In other words, risk-reduction mechanisms must be implemented to leverage capital from standard money markets and use them to promote the growth of private enterprise in the ghetto.

Cross observes that the ghetto economy does not obey the rules of the larger economy; he calls it "economic anarchy." In times of plenty in the general economy, the ghetto goes backward and unemployment rises. This is because the white-dominated institutions will only employ blacks if a suitable white is not available; history shows that the only times for high minority employment have been during major wars of this country. The ghetto is characterized by unavailable or exorbitant credit, high crime rates, low median disposable incomes, small savings (a source of equity capital), high insurance rates, and limited support institutions. In other words, all the normal incentives to business formation are missing. Therefore, the ghetto cannot be treated as a reflection of the larger economy. The palliatives given in the past, such as welfare, jobs programs, and the like, do not attack the root cause of ghetto poverty, namely, *the lack of viable capital formation and retention institutions.*

Cross feels that the ghetto is fundamentally structured to prevent the accumulation of wealth because it:

1. is inhospitable to investment or technical assistance;
2. provides little motivation to save or convert even available savings to venture capital;
3. offers little or no entrepreneural opportunity in legitimate business; and,
4. is isolated from the mainstream economy by a series of tariffs on retail sales, rents, and credit, but is totally dependent on imports from the mainstream economy for most of their basic goods and services.[4]

Cross therefore feels that the economic system of the ghetto economy militates against traditional programs of welfare or charity as a vehicle for change. He concludes that the federal government has been unable to demonstrate competence in implementing anti-poverty programs. Hence, he recommends a system of federal incentives, guarantees, and subsidies that will induce a massive infusion of private capital and know-how into the ghettos. These capital-creation mechanisms will initiate the formation of viable capital retention institutions, which in turn will generate more capital via the multiplier effect. These mechanisms must be structured to provide a compelling rationale for private investment, not one based on charity or guilt feelings.

Cross assumes that OFC will test various financial incentives and demonstrate their worth in moving capital into the ghetto. Once such a facility is appropriately demonstrated, legislation can be initiated to create a multi-million-dollar national minority funding corporation with the economic clout really to create social change.

In contrast, Sharon Lockwood, Economic Advisor to the President's Advisory Council for Minority Business Enterprise (PACME) and Financial Economist for the Small Business Administration, believes that the economic system in the ghetto operates quite rationally but by its own set of rules, not in the manner of "economic anarchy" as Cross states. She contends firmly that it is not a malfunctioning anarchy, but it is simply different because it operates under a different logic system. Cross, to prove his point on the "anarchy" issue, argues that blacks and other minorities buy a disproportionate amount of prepared food (which is more expensive than unprepared), thereby exhibiting their economic irrationality. Lockwood, on the other hand, contends that this behavior is supremely rational by the logic of the ghetto. For example, the ghetto resident typically does not enjoy the middle-class conveniences of stoves and refrigerators and, as a result, is forced to eat prepared foods.

This disagreement, substantial though it may be, is no cause in and of itself to discredit Cross' pioneering work. However, it does point up the fact that, perhaps, Cross was somewhat naive in his assumptions that financial incentives alone would move substantial capital into the ghetto as well as they had moved it into the mainstream economy.

THE CREATION OF THE OPPORTUNITY FUNDING CORPORATION

The Early Negotiations
The early negotiations for the OEO grant to OFC were conducted at the OEO office in Washington. The difficulties with the negotiations centered mainly around two questions:

1. How were the OFC programs to be evaluated?
2. How was OFC to be funded?

Goal Determination and Strategy
In the early negotiations, two different philosophies of the OFC experiment were considered. The first was that OFC would be a vehicle for experimentation with a variety of incentives; the second was that OFC *itself* was the thing being tested. (Is this organizational form the desirable type of

mechanism for testing programs?) Stated differently, the dichotomy was between evaluating different experiments and evaluating a prototype of an institution to assist minority business.

OFC wanted as much flexibility as possible in making deals and trying out the incentives. Overall goals were rather loosely worded and diffuse. For each program, the proposal submitted to OEO for approval spelled out the specific program goals. Just as OFC wanted flexibility, OEO wanted to tie down the program to specific carefully worded goal statements for evaluation purposes.

President of OFC, Jack Gloster, experienced in government bureaucracies through his several years in the State Department, was familiar with the problems associated with implementing innovative programs in a federal agency context and recognized the pressure for early successes in agency programs for refunding reasons. Therefore, he chose to delay the implementation of the more complicated and potentially more risky programs until a "track record" of success was generated.

In October 1972, a major reclarification of OFC's goals was formulated:

> OFC programs and projects are selected for their potential for demonstrating successful and innovative application of these techniques, *and* for their likely impact upon the economic development of low-income communities. In considering the *economic development impact,* OFC gives particular weight to a project's potential for expanding ownership opportunities among the poor, affording significant opportunities for expanded employment and job development increasing capital accumulation among the poor, and strengthening of institutions which can have a multiplier effect upon the economies of low-income communities. In this sense, as well as because of its emphasis upon replicability and demonstration value, OFC differs from other programs and organizations which have as their primary goal minority business development. While we are of course concerned that the ventures we assist have the potential of business viability, we are also concerned that they offer the prospect of significant economic impact upon a relatively broad segment of the poverty community.

From the principles just described OFC has derived the following long-term goals:

1. To test the effectiveness of indirect financing techniques (guarantees, secondary marketing arrangements, incentive subsidies) in increasing the amounts of *investment capital* available for economic development activities in low-income communities;
2. To test the effectiveness of these techniques in increasing the availability of working capital in these communities;

3. To test whether, through the increased availability of capital, new and existing institutions can be made more effective instruments of economic development in low-income communities;
4. To test whether or not increased availability of investment and working capital can make a significant impact upon the pace of economic development in low-income communities.

> Obviously OFC's ability to meet the latter two of these goals depends upon attaining positive results from the first two. That is, only if the indirect financing techniques are successful in attracting investment and working capital will we be able to measure the effect of that new capital on institution-building and the pace of community economic development.[5]

Structure and Funding

The Opportunity Funding Corporation was to be a non-profit organization, funded by OEO Title ID and research and demonstration monies. This Washington-based corporation would be sparsely staffed at first: a president, a vice president for program development, a vice president for research and evaluation, an executive assistant to the president, and an administrative officer, with all but one being black. OFC has since added a vice president for program management (white), a general counsel (black), and a director of communications (white).

As discussed in the previous chapter, OEO is primarily a social welfare agency, having only recently entered the minority economic development field—and then only in a small way. OFC is somewhat of a stranger to the OEO fold for this reason. OFC is not designed to transfer money to either poor people or to groups representing poor people; rather, it uses its $7.1 million in venture capital funds (the remaining $300,000 of its total of $7.4 million in funding being used for administrative expenses) as an experimentation/demonstration program in order to test a variety of financial incentives in a number of rural and urban settings. As will become clear later in this study, this goal is not perceived the same way by all actors in the OFC evaluation environment. As discussed in the Statement of Work for OFC, the corporation was to design programs that allow for field evaluation in order to determine the optimal strategy mix of incentives.

The various programs were divided rather informally among the OFC vice presidents. For example, the Surety Bonding Program was placed under Paul Pryde, the vice president for program development. The Banking Program, the LDC/SBA 502 Program, and a portion of the Flexible Guarantee Program fell under Steve Nelson, vice president for research and evaluation. Pryde also handles the Real Estate Program and the new Consumer Credit Program (not implemented). Arnold Nachmanoff, vice president for program management, has primary responsibility for the Flexible Guarantee Program.

Early in the "Project X" days, the structure of OFC was not determined. Some OEO personnel felt control would be easier if OEO implemented the programs and never created a separate OFC. However, according to Carol Khosrovi (Director of EDD) a separate entity was created for these reasons:

> You may ask: Why an independent, non-profit corporation as the OFC model? There are never enough people at OEO to launch a project of this size and scope. Also, Rumsfeld distrusted the OEO staff. He felt they were a bunch of liberal free-swinging Democrats. He felt the bureaucracy would sabotage him. He liked the OFC model because he felt we should test a model with business people guiding it, not government bureaucrats.
>
> *Don Lowitz* disagrees: It is true that there were frictions between the old staff and the new administration at OEO, but the reason OFC was never seriously considered as an "in house" project had to have a separate entity with distinguished directors, etc. In addition, of course, the size of the project clearly indicated that OEO could never have sufficient staff to do justice to this project and still carry out its other functions. We were primarily interested in testing a model project which we hoped would have a financial impact on the poor community. OFC was this model and we were dedicated to establishing it in a way which would provide for the most meaningful test.

The Board of Directors

The selection of the board was a very informal process. Ted Cross, Sam Doctors, Don Lowitz, Bill Walker (an aide to Rumsfeld) and Donald Rumsfeld himself spent many hours brainstorming about potential candidates. (A difference of opinion exists between Sam Doctors and Don Lowitz as to whether these nominations were cleared with the White House; Lowitz denies that they were.) The board was selected with an eye toward OFC's desired independence from outside influence, including the federal government. To accomplish this, a strong and prestigious board was essential. The members of the first board were:

Dr. David Hertz, chairman (director, McKinsey and Co.);
Robert O. Dehlendorf II (president, Arcata National Corporation);
Eli Goldston (president, Eastern Gas and Fuel Association);
James M. Hall (secretary, Business and Transportation Agency, State of California);
Dan Lufkin (chairman, executive committee, Donaldson, Lufkin);
John Mabie (vice-president and director, A.G. Becker Corporation);
Alex Mercure (state project director, Project HELP, Albuquerque)—Chicano member;

Rev. Leon Sullivan (president, Opportunities Industrialization Center)—black
member

Dr. Robert Vowels (dean, School of Business Administration, Atlanta University)—black member.

The board was considered to be fairly evenly divided among
Republicans and Democrats. More importantly, it was composed of men who
were conscious of the inequities in this country yet still believed that capitalism
is a viable vehicle to obtain economic parity of sorts. The logic was that
if the poor learn the rules of the game, they can be just as successful at playing
it as have been middle-class Americans.

The board has changed its composition slowly. Leon Sullivan asked
to be replaced (in 1972) since his duties as a General Motors board member
took up too much of his time. Dr. Jesse Jay, superintendent of Knox County
Schools, Barbourville, Kentucky, was added to give representation in the white
disadvantaged community of Appalachia, and Nathan T. Garrett, executive
director of the Foundation for Community Development, Inc., Durham, North
Carolina, was added to give a community development perspective (both in
September 1971). J. Howard Marshall II, director of the Texas Commerce
Bank, Houston, Texas, gives the Board valuable financial experienced joined
the board in 1972.

Two women, Carol M. Khosrovi (1973) (consultant) and Dolores
C. Tucker (1972) (Pennsylvania Secretary of State), were added as were the
executive vice president of a Denver bank, Theodore D. Brown (1973) and
Arthur R. Taylor (1973) President, Columbia Broadcasting System. David
Hertz remains as board chairman, and in 1972 John Mable was appointed vice
chairman.

Board attendance has been somewhat irregular, with geographical
dispersion and busy schedules contributing to this problem. For the first year,
board meetings were held every other month, with the Finance and Investment
Committee (the committee that decides investment policy and reserves policy)
meeting in between these regular board meetings. While all members have not
attended every meeting, there have only been two instances of failure to make
a quorum.

After substantial interviewing, Jack Gloster was chosen by the
Board as its president. Gloster began his duties in November 1970.

Relationship of OFC to OEO

At a very basic level, OEO and OFC appear to have conflicting
foci. According to Mike Brazzel:

> The focus of OEO techniques and approach is on the community.
> OFC is not community focused; rather, it is a financial organization, not people oriented. This is an alien notion to OEO.[6]

Because of this alleged lack of sympathy for OFC purposes, Brazzel indicated that OEO did not take the OFC project seriously. But, according to Lowitz:

> I feel there has been an overemphasis of an antagonistic relationship between OEO and OFC. As I view it, both parties were doing their jobs. We at OEO sought to create a project that met the prerequisites of the Economic Opportunity Act and still gave OFC a free reign to 'do its thing.' OFC sought as much autonomy as possible. In the end I was satisfied that both OEO and OFC had put together a grant that resolved any differences in this area.

The relationship, then, between the two organizations was hardly relaxed and informal. Rather, they seemed to be actual or potential antagonists in most of their interactions. The "control over the experiments" issue was merely a manifestation of this original antagonistic relationship. The OEO officials demanded, on the Statement of Work for OFC's formation, that they get final review authority over any OFC program so that the experimental design would be adequate.

THE OPERATION OF THE OPPORTUNITY
FUNDING CORPORATION

Initial and Current Program Components

The original conception of the OFC organization was in three program components:

1. *Opportunity Guaranty Component:* guarantees to attract capital into low-income communities;
2. *Community Development Discount Component:* establish secondary markets for SBA and EDA-backed obligations; and,
3. *Incentive Stimulator Component:* to test various incentives (i.e., tax incentives) in their ability to attract capital in low-income areas.

The organization of OFC was originally to be structured around these components but, after forming the organization, it was found that the organization could be structured in a more effective manner. Each of these components is still alive as either an operational OFC program or a soon-to-be implemented program.

OFC, as an experimentation/demonstration program, should be insuring that an accurate and scientific evaluation of its programs takes place on a timely basis. Because of the operational priority of the OFC staff (and a concomitant lower priority of the evaluation issue), the emphasis is more on performance of making "good deals"; data collection and analysis for the purpose of acquiring generalizable information is a lesser concern. The OFC team is mainly concerned with flexibility—the ability to seize the financial opportunity. They have a tendency to see OEO and its evaluation emphasis as impediments to the smooth functioning of the organization.

Surety Bonding Program

The first major OFC program to be implemented was the minority contractor's Surety Bonding Program. This is a demonstration project that tests various financial incentives for improving the competitive position of minority contractors within the low-income community. Surety bonding is a formidable obstacle to minority contractors. While racism may be partly to blame, lack of bonding is primarily a reflection of the contractor's weak financial condition and unestablished track record.

The technological advances in the construction industry, accompanied by increasing economies of scale, tend to place small minority contractors at a disadvantage. To qualify for bonding and to have a reasonable chance for financial success, minority contractors must overcome racial prejudice as well as problems of insufficient working capital, limited access to a qualified labor force, and minimal expertise in such crucial areas as management, cost accounting, cost estimation, and bidding. To help alleviate these problems, OFC proposes to demonstrate that various financial devices (such as guarantees) can be judiciously used as a means of reducing the perceived risk. OFC hopes to show that these devices will leverage many times their worth in financial and technical assistance from the private sector. In collaboration with the Minority Contractors Assistance Program (MCAP), OFC also plans to help get management and technical assistance to the minority contractor involved, especially in the critical early stages of each project.

Wocala, Inc., of Visalia, California, was a Chicano-owned reforestation firm that employed primarily migrant labor and had both government (U.S. Department of Forestry) and private (Weyerhauser) contracts. OFC had issued Wocala a $25,000 letter of credit in favor of surety companies which had agreed to issue performance bonds totaling $125,000 and bid bonds of $250,000. As of July 1, 1972, more than $175,000 of work in process had accrued to the $25,000 OFC bond (for which OFC has a $17,000 reserve) for a leverage factor of over 10:1.

Subsequently, Wocala encountered serious financial difficulties. The possibility of a loss under OFC's $25,000 Letter of Credit to Fidelity and Deposit Insurance Company seemed high, but it was subsequently determined that all of the contracts covered by OFC's Letter of Credit were completed, and therefore no significant loss was sustained. Wocala itself has been dissolved as an operating company, and a case study has been prepared by Steve Nelson to illuminate the learning experience for OFC from the Wocala relationship.

Other OFC Surety Bonding projects include:

1. Oglala Sioux—$60,000 reserve commitment for $1.3 million in funds generated, or leverage of 21:1;
2. Glemit Construction Company—$11,500 in reserve has generated $67,000 in business for leverage of 6:1;
3. Industrialized Business Systems (IBSC)—$1000,000 reserve has generated $1.7 million in funds for leverage of 17:1;
4. Equity Development Corporation—$45,000 reserve for $100,000 in initial capitalization, or a leverage factor of over 2:1;
5. P & P Construction Company—$10,250 reserve for $153,500 for leverage of 15:1.

Equity Development also has been in serious financial trouble. Although the firm sustained losses on its first two projects, OFC's guarantee that provided Equity's initial funding has not been called upon. According to Nelson, Equity has received substantial new projects and contracts that may permit it to recoup its losses. The OFC Board, however, has decided to maintain the reserves on this project at 100 percent.

In May of 1971, an OFC staff member met with representatives of IBSC, the black modular construction firm that was able to obtain bonding for a $1.7 million project with an OFC guaranty, and he visited the site of the construction. The project, a low-income housing development, appears to be on schedule.

Glemit Construction Company in Atlanta successfully completed its contract to pave an FAA parking lot, and OFC's $17,000 guaranty expired on schedule on May 15, 1972.

The Oglala Sioux Tribal Building Enterprise completed the first phase of the turnkey housing project that was financed with the help of an OFC Letter of Credit. The Sioux sustained a small loss in the first phase, but they expect to recover upon completion of the second phase, which will be subcontracted to an established builder. OFC's guaranty will remain in force until profits from the second phase are sufficient to pay off the bank loan.

There are some points of theory that are essential to an understanding of this program. The first of these is the concept of the time value of money. Since there is an opportunity cost associated with money, the faster you can turn it over, the more efficiently it will work for you. Therefore, in the Bonding and other OFC programs, the size of the reserve requirement (how much you have tied up) is important, but equally important is the *duration of the commitment of that reserve.* If, as in the Glemit case, OFC can turn its reserves over rapidly, it will gain more efficiency from its venture capital and generate more leverage. Leverage is the other point of theory that needs clarification. Leverage, simply stated, is the funds generated by a specific financial technique divided by the expenses associated with implementing that technique.

However, it is sometimes difficult to decide on the precise definition of leverage, and this is a crucial decision as it reflects the "success" or "failure" of a given technique. OFC has recently published a definition of leverage for its programs.[7] However, there is still a need for more analysis of this concept, particularly with regard to the use of "time" in the measurement of the leverage.

p.84

The Banking Program

The second OFC program to be implemented was the Banking Program. A five-pronged apporach, the Banking Program seeks to increase deposits in poverty-area banks (direct deposits and incentives to encourage deposits), to stimulate capital infusion, to create a secondary market for SBA-guaranteed paper, and to develop the management capabilities of poverty-area banking officers and directors.

Direct Deposit Support.   In this approach, OFC has placed a substantial portion of its uncommitted venture capital (currently around $5.5 million) in time deposits and open-demand deposits in more than forty poverty-area banks. This action increases the deposit position for these small banks and gives them funds to pump into the disadvantaged community in the form of business and consumer loans, thereby promoting economic development. One of the requirements for banks' accepting OFC deposits is that each bank agrees to attempt to invest at least 60 percent of the amount deposited by OFC into new loans to businesses, community organizations, or consumers located in or doing most of their business in the poverty community served by that bank. OFC has committed $97,020 in reserves to generate $3,430,000 for leverage of 35:1.

Indirect Deposit Support.   This approach has two elements—deposit guarantees and interest subsidies. OFC may selectively guarantee that portion of deposits made in minority banks that exceeds the FDIC insurance limit of $20,000; such guarantees will be made up to a total of $50,000 in any given instance (an OFC exposure of $30,000). The Interest Subsidy technique will be used in two ways:

1. To compensate investors for gaps which may exist between rates paid by participating poverty-area banks and those paid on comparable investments in competing white banks;
2. To provide for the selective payment of *premium* rates to test the effectiveness of such added risk-compensation incentives in attracting deposits.[8]

OFC is planning for the future implementation of its Indirect Deposit Program at selected minority banks. This project has been placed on the "back burner" in terms of OFC program implementation priorities.

Capital Support.   OFC recognizes three widely differing types of circumstances that often require minority banks to raise capital. The first, particularly common for new banks, occurs when the institution incurs larger than anticipated losses through insufficient lending experience, high personnel expenses, or both. The second situation is more often characteristic of older institutions and arises when the bank experiences rapid deposit growth and/or when it needs to expand its facilities (e.g., establishment of branch operations). The final situation comes in the establishment of a new bank. In each of these situations, the bank may find it difficult to raise new capital, operating as it does in the capital-poor ghetto economy. Under these circumstances, it will almost certainly find it necessary to introduce some risk-reduction feature to attract outside capital. OFC may provide capital note guarantees or other arrangements (such as interest subsidy payments on capital notes or debentures) to overcome the reluctance of the outside investor to participate in such stock issues. The following are two specific examples of OFC Capital Support.

The Unity Bank Case.   Unity Bank and Trust Company of Boston opened its doors in June 1968 with an initial capitalization of $1,000,000, approximately 65 percent of which came from the black community in Roxbury, Massachusetts. By December 1970, Unity had begun experiencing excessive losses through the steady deterioration of its loan portfolio as well as high personnel costs resulting from excessive turnover and heavy training cost for inexperienced personnel. As a consequence, its capital base became somewhat impaired. A series of negotiations between a group of Boston banks, Unity officials, OFC, and the Massachusetts Bankers Association culminated with an arrangement whereby four large Boston banks put up $400,000 and the Massachusetts Bankers Association agreed to put up $100,000. This $500,000 capital support was 80 percent guaranteed by OFC ($200,000), the Cooperative Assistance Fund ($100,000), and Interracial Council for Business Opportunities (ICBO) ($100,000). OFC, on behalf of the guarantors, would agree to retain in its portfolio specific certificates of deposit equal to the amount of the guarantee for the life of the loan and would additionally agree to pledge income from $300,000 of its certificate as collateral as such income was realized.

This led to the additional infusion of capital notes in the amount of $1,500,000 by the FDIC, with a contingency infusion of another $500,000, if needed. This role of the FDIC, committing itself to providing funds for the recapitalization of an insured bank, was unprecedented. FDIC found its legal basis for this unusual intervention in a long unused rule permitting it to take such action in a situation in which the bank in question was the only bank serving its community. In this case, FDIC took the stance that Roxbury was an identifiable community and that Unity was the only bank whose major objective was to serve that predominantly black community.

OFC's role in this deal was that of a catalyst and coordinator. It helped negotiate the terms and conditions of the total financial infusion to Unity. OFC's guarantee was essentially leveraged to a $2 million capital support, or a 30 to 1 leverage factor (the actual dollar cost to OFC is only the opportunity cost involved in the maintenance of a $67,000 reserve), plus the time involved in putting the deal together. This deal was consummated on July 27, 1971, and the bank is doing quite well thus far.

OFC has other strategies for loan guarantees that it hopes to use in the future. The following hypothetical example shows how one such strategy might work. The stock of a bank will be sold at $30 per share, with OFC giving a "put" at 60 percent of the stock price ($18), the equivalent of a 60 percent guarantee, to the purchasers of the stock (e.g., a community organization). Also, OFC will take a "call" on the stock at purchase price plus estimated resale expense or $32.50 per share. This provision would be handy in the event that the purchased stock was to be re-sold to the community residents by the organization; the "call" would insure this re-sale. This rather sophisticated strategy is a potential model for future OFC Capital Support operations.

The Midwest Bank Case. [9]   Midwest National Bank of Indianapolis opened its doors on October 3, 1972. In a number of respects this new black owned bank represents an inspiring model for many communities seeking to organize their own banks.

Recognizing the need for sufficient capital to survive the early "learning period" of Midwest Bank's history, the organizers had decided to raise initial capital of $2,000,000 through the sale of 80,000 shares of common stock at $25 per share. When Midwest contacted OFC, approximately $1 million of the authorized common had been sold to nearly 1,200 members of the Indianapolis black community. An additional $500,000 had been subscribed by locally based white-owned corporations and another $100,000 by an Indiana foundation. While additional equity could probably have been sold within the local white community, Midwest's organizers were reluctant to do so because they believed it to be essential to the success of the bank to maintain community confidence that the bank was in fact black-controlled.

Through contact with the National Urban Coalition, one of the organizers approached OFC and the Cooperative Assistance Fund (CAF was established as a separate foundation by six major foundations to provide funds on minority economic development) for help in arranging for sale of the remaining $300,000 of common stock. Both organizations were impressed by the substantial progress achieved by Midwest in identifying and committing experienced management for the bank, selecting and acquiring a highly desirable and accessible site on a primary thoroughfare, obtaining an imaginative and functional architectural design for the bank building and, most of all, raising 80 percent of the projected capitalization locally with 50 percent from the black community itself. Both OFC and CAF were also impressed by the bank's broad base of ownership, with no single investor holding more than 10 percent of the authorized shares. CAF's president agreed to recommend to his Investment Committee that CAF purchase $100,000 of the remaining stock.[10] After exploring the nature of OFC's guarantee authorities, Midwest's organizers expressed confidence that with the additional backing of OFC guarantees, Indiana National Bank would be willing to make facilitative loans to members of the organizing group to enable them to purchase the final 8,000 shares.

For OFC, this proposal represented an opportunity to determine what type of guarantee arrangement might be successful in the capitalization of a *new* minority bank. Therefore, at its November, 1971 meeting, OFC's Investment Committee authorized the president to attempt to negotiate acceptable guarantee arrangements to permit purchase of the remaining authorized stock.

Subsequently OFC entered into negotiations with Indiana National through the bank's counsel, David Givens. On March 29, 1972, OFC's president and general counsel and CAF's president, with representatives of Midwest, met with Mr. Givens, and it was learned that Indiana National had provided loans for the first $200,000 in shares purchased by the organizers.

On May 8, final arrangements were concluded on the basis of OFC's last proposal, guaranteeing 40 percent of each individual loan for four years, and guarantee documents were signed for notes totaling $153,000. This represented the amount then needed for stock purchases to total $2,000,000, and completed the capitalization of Midwest National. OFC had used reserves of $20,400 for the $2,000,000 generated for a leverage factor of 98:1.

Liquidity Enhancement. In this approach, the idea is to test the ability of an outside vehicle (OFC) to increase the lending capacity of poverty-area banks by buying the insured portion of SBA or other insured loans and remarketing them. If this can be done successfully with commercial bank paper, OFC may attempt to extend this principle in subsequent programs to loans originated by credit unions, community development corporations, and other poverty-area lending institutions. OFC is exploring ways of creating a secondary market for such discounted paper. Pending the development of such a market (as well as for short periods while arranging placement after the market is developed), it is anticipated that OFC may hold such paper in its own portfolio. This project has also been placed on the "back burner" of OFC program implementation plans.

Management Development. The final Banking Program segment is the management development approach. Using the interest generated by the direct deposit program certificates of deposit (CDs), OFC plans to develop and implement a Management Development Project for lending officers and directors of minority banks. The program will consist of seminars conducted in regional areas near the banks or at the banks themselves. This project is being developed under the sponsorship of the National Bankers Association (the minority banks' professional organization), with the cooperation of the American Bankers Association, certain educational institutions, and others. The first phase, a seminar for participating bank directors and senior officers, was conducted on July 20–22, 1973, in Atlanta. Ed Irons, former NBA director, assisted in the development and the implementation of both phases of the project; the second phase will provide on-site technical and management assistance to key bank officials.

New OFC Programs

A third major program, the SBA 502/LDC local injection project, permits OFC to back up local groups by raising the 10 percent local matching contribution for SBA plant and facilities loans. OFC is again acting as a catalyst and leveraging agent in using existing government programs and the resources of different organizations to put the deal together. Churches had been infusing millions into minority communities but they had been "burned"; in other words, they had taken a loss. OFC, through the successful 502 program, is now talking to Jewish, Methodist, and Catholic groups to get their money back into the economic mainstream to aid minority economic development. A major project in New Jersey and New York is in process. The first transaction involves the Presbyterian Economic Development Corporation (PEDCO), which is making $400,000 available (subject to OFC guarantees).

In theory, this $400,000 could provide up to $4,000,000 in leverage. This OFC support means crucially needed front-end money for several local development corporations. Current PEDCO minority investment projects include:

1. An upholstering firm—$4,750 in OFC reserves has generated $95,000 or leverage of 20:1;
2. A sheetmetal manufacturer—$4,000 has generated $80,000 for 20:1;
3. A furniture store—$8,000 generates $160,000.

In total, OFC has reserves of $48,700 generating $1,114,400 for a leverage of 23:1.

The Flexible Guarantee Program. Two other programs (Flexible Guarantee and Real Estate) were approved by the OFC Board of Directors at a meeting on February 24, 1972, and subsequently have been approved by OEO officials. In the flexible guarantee program, OFC proposes to alleviate a critical problem regarding the federal guarantee of building projects—that is, the inflexibility of the terms of SBA or other government guarantees. For example, SBA guarantees are all issued at the maximum rate allowable, which is 90 percent of the loan. As explained earlier, this unnecessarily ties up government monies in reserve for guarantees, since many minority projects have smaller risk factors wherein much lower guarantee levels could be negotiated. This reduces the leverage factor for government funds by providing lower turnover of money in guarantees.

In addition, SBA loans are restricted as to types of lenders and borrowers who are acceptable. Interminable red tape and delays are the rule, rather than the exception. Time-consuming forms must be filled out, sometimes necessitating outside technical assistance. Frequently, SBA will not allow a deal involving more than one type of institution. However, it often takes the cooperation of several institutions, each with its own bureaucracy, to put a deal together. A private lending agency may incur high costs by participating in SBA loans due to the red tape and time involved. The reason SBA inflexibility is so important is that more than half of the $500 million spent in fiscal year 1972 on minority economic development came from SBA, either in the form of loans to MESBICs, loan guarantees, direct loans, or the 8(a) minority procurement program. This is a crucial agency in minority economic development, and in many ways, it is not meeting the needs of the minority community.

This government inflexibility is particularly damaging to minority economic development since fewer projects can be started with a given guarantee pool. The main issue, however, is the fact that 90 percent guarantees are *not* necessary for all poverty-area projects; some are not at all risky, and the lender could easily be protected by a substantially lower guarantee. Another factor is leverage; SBA leverage is typically only 4:1. OFC anticipates that through the use of flexible guarantees, leverage factors of 20:1 and greater will be generated.

Through the use of flexible (negotiable) guarantees, OFC hopes that more poverty-area projects can safely be initiated with a given amount of funds. OFC will have the flexibility to work either alone or with a community organization "partner" to put together financial packages of high complexity that cannot be consummated through existing federal programs. This direct contact with community organizations is a big plus for the OFC approach. SBA can make loans only to profit-making entities, thereby excluding community development corporations and other community organizations closely attuned to community needs and problems. OFC, working through a community "partner," will be able to gauge the pulse of the community and negotiate deals important to the development of the community.

Real Estate Program.   The Real Estate Program has interesting potential. In low-income communities, real estate values are disproportionately low; abandoned buildings present an eyesore as well as a hazard for residents. This has a domino effect which results in a reduced tax base that adversely affects community services. The development of real estate has high potential for providing immediate income for persons involved in various facets of this activity. Construction and renovation of residences and commercial property provides many jobs for contractors and laborers. This increase may be obtained with maximum leverage because the collateralized value of real property typically permits the use of very high proportions of borrowed money. Thus, an owner (such as a community organization) may be able to obtain construction of a building with an initial equity that represents only a small fraction of the total building price.

Most of the advantages of real estate development are widely known, yet there are no federal programs specifically designed to facilitate real estate development by low-income community organizations. There are many sources of funds for development, both public and private. However, community organizations find their "high-risk" status and lack of expertise often prohibits access to these funds. At present, the numerous leveraging possibilities inherent in real estate development serve only to benefit those who understand the intricacies of real estate financing and development, have experience in the area, and have a large net worth. OFC intends to demonstrate, with the aid of guarantees, that low-income communities can circumvent these "rights of entry" barriers. This demonstration project will then serve as a basis for recommending changes in existing federal programs (e.g., EDA, GNMA, SBA), including possible legislation.

Targets for Funding

OFC's stated purpose is to test the effectiveness of various incentive techniques in attracting private sources of money in rural and urban low-income areas. Each of the pilot projects is designed to establish a specific need for a legislative and/or administrative change. OFC chose four criteria for the selection of projects for assistance:

1. The project must be innovative in concept and must provide leverage for OFC's assistance.
2. The project must have national impact. (This is a source of conflict; OFC wants national impact but has a budget of $7.1 million, and the two are incompatible).
3. The project must be capable of being reproduced in other localities.
4. The project must have demonstrable benefits for poverty-area residents.

Difficulties with the OFC Concept

There are many potential problems that OFC has experienced and will continue to experience. The early damage to OFC by the secret, elitist

"Project X" has won them many opponents among CDC personnel and in the minority community. Because of the low current level of funding, OFC says that it will be able to initiate only one or two experiments at the same time in a given ghetto area. There is disagreement on this question—Hertz believes that OFC could plan for an impact area and implement many programs simultaneously. With OFC's priority of helping minority business, they could strike where there is interest, not necessarily in the same geographic area, and make deals that have a reasonable chance of success.

Cross, in *Black Capitalism,* talks about achieving financial synergy by concentrating several programs in a given area by, for example, making loan guarantees, rediscounting SBA paper and creating a secondary market for it, stimulating deposits in slum-area banks, increasing the amount of venture capital available to ghetto entrepreneurs, and planning other programs to develop ghettos. This synergy will probably never be achieved under the current OFC design.

Measurement of results will be difficult. For example, in the Banking Program it is impossible to separate out the effect of a $5.5 million deposit program when the public/private $100 million deposit program was going on simultaneously.[11] Given the complexity of the development process in general, the additional problems of operating in a ghetto environment, and adding the lukewarm feeling of OFC toward evaluation, there is little hope that superior evaluations can be performed.

There is an emphasis on short-term results in federal demonstration programs, and OFC is no exception. In the early stages the political pressures were very strong, so OFC necessarily opted for low-risk projects that were not very innovative, especially in the early days. However, the pressure has diminished because of Board intervention with various governmental officials and because of OEO administrative chances. However, OFC must show the CDCs that it does leverage its funding, or it will come under increasing attack from that quarter. OFC must justify its existence; it must show that it can do things which no existing federal program can do.

Another problem area is the transferability of results of successful experiments to operating agencies. The technology transfer problem has not been looked at in any detail by the OFC staff. In fact, one of the officers has mentioned that it is conceivable that successful experimentation will lead to increased funding and the establishment of a national funding corporation (an operating entity). This assumption precludes the problem of worrying about the transfer of technology to other government agencies.

Continued funding will be difficult in any event, given the general administration motivational feeling to cut back OEO funding. This is one reason why OFC is searching at this moment for additional sources of funding (e.g., Ford Foundation and OMBE). Another reason for seeking other funding sources is to reduce OFC's funding dependence upon a single sponsor.

The whole question about who should control the experiments still has not fully been resolved. The OEO evaluation orientation clashes with the operations orientation of OFC and will continue to do so in the present environment. OEO does keep a tight rein on OFC with regard to evaluation, but, in comparison to other OEO–grantees, OFC has significantly more freedom. In any event, there is a continuing need to balance the goals of the two organizations to insure maximum flexibility to experiment for OFC while allowing OEO to maintain a reasonable amount of direction and control over the experiments, which would thus ensure good feedback for other OEO programs and for transfer to various operating agencies. Whether this balance can be achieved realistically remains to be seen.

EVOLUTION OF THE EVALUATION FUNCTION

Cross is a free-wheeling and aggressive type of businessman as illustrated by an early "Project X" memorandum:

> The president of OFC should be a member of the Board of Directors and preferably have very broad powers under the articles and charter to hire and fire staff; obligate the agency up to a relatively high limit (say $100,000) without going to the Board; hire consultants as needed; negotiate contracts with other agencies and foundations.

Cross instinctively knew that such a posture would get OFC in trouble with the evaluation-conscious OEO. Therefore, Cross was careful to point up the need of constantly assuaging OEO's feelings in this regard:

> A continuing, informal, informative, friendly relationship must be established with the evaluation group at OEO. The evaluation function is crucial in measuring program impact and for public relations. Several independent evaluations of OFC projects might be purchased by OFC to supplement the official evaluation programs.

However, according to Nelson, OFC's administrative budget is a strict line item budget, and there is no room for flexibility by Gloster in allocating the funds to different areas of need (including evaluation). There are currently no funds specifically set aside for evaluation in the OFC administrative budget; however, Nelson has indicated that OFC will probably petition OEO for funds to conduct the semi-annual self-evaluation requested by Louis Ramirez, new director of EDD.

OEO's Response to the Cross Position

As was pointed out earlier, OEO considered OFC somewhat of a stepchild. Regardless of this somewhat haphazard approach to the evaluation of the OFC experiments in the formative stages, OEO finally did get down to some hard negotiating over the evaluation issue. Tony Partridge (OEO counsel), Don Lowitz, and Bob Bicks (New York City attorney representing OFC), and Ted Cross sat down together for many hours and worked out a compromise Statement of Work. Cross, of course, was vitally concerned with flexibility (the ability to negotiate deals as the opportunity presents itself), a reasonable degree of autonomy from OEO (for reasons of control), and an assurance that program approval would not be slowed interminably by government red tape.

The OFC Evaluation Orientation

There are some indications that the OFC position was altered in the 1971-72 period. One OFC board member argues that, while Gloster is a "little opportunistic" at times, OFC is now moving into a phase of learning and experimenting and out of a phase where short-term results were paramount.[12] Another board member confirms this fact, adding that the board has always stressed evaluation to the OFC management.

The Role of the Northwestern Consultants In the Evaluation Function

In June 1971, a group of Northwestern University professors and graduate students working under the corporation, Economic Innovations, Inc., were retained by OFC as consultants. The first project was to develop a general evaluation strategy for OFC. In addition, Economic Innovations was asked to design or re-design the evaluation portion of each of the following programs: Banking, Surety Bonding, SBA 502/LDC, Flexible Guarantee, Real Estate, and Consumer Credit.

At first, OFC was very enthusiastic about the potential role of Economic Innovations. The consultants were instructed to "produce the best possible evaluation design for our experiments." OFC appeared to be very conscious of the necessity for a rigorous evaluation of its programs. However, the limitations imposed on OFC by its lack of an evaluation budget and the need to move programs rapidly to the implementation stage led to a refinement of OFC's evaluation philosophy.

With these constraints, OFC re-examined its position on the evaluation issue and began to articulate a definitive position in this area. As a result, Economic Innovations, Inc., was instructed to design evaluations "good enough to satisfy OEO." This was not to imply that OFC was totally uninterested in evaluation; it does indicate that on a priority basis, the implementation of successful programs and the re-funding of OFC transcended evaluation considerations. More correctly, where supporting evaluation could enhance the achievement of the first two goals, OFC was strongly pro-evaluation; where the goals were not an issue, evaluation was still supported by OFC, but with less enthusiasm. When asked by an Economic Innovations member to identify the target of the proposed strategy document, Nelson replied:

> Its first job is to satisfy OEO. Secondly, it is needed to give OFC direction. We can learn from the evaluation of failures as well as successes, but, for budgetary reasons, we need short-term successes. The most important thing to remember is that OFC needs as much flexibility as possible in the general evaluation strategy.

The input of Economic Innovations, Inc., to the OFC operation steadily decreased till the end of 1972 when it was terminated entirely. This appears to be due, in part, to a very small budget item for consulting expenses, to be exact, a total of $30,000 for nineteen months. In addition, OFC is trying to increase its in-house capability for designing programs and their evaluation, thereby reducing their dependency on outside consultants.

The Boone-Young Relationship to OFC
Boone, Young and Associates, a black consulting firm in New York City, was employed by OEO to evaluate OFC's Surety Bonding Program.

Boone-Young submitted an interim report of progress on the Surety Bonding evaluation to OEO as of March 31, 1972. It is a narrative about the Minority Contractors Assistance Program (MCAP) and OFC's relationship to it, together with descriptions of various MCAP affiliates. There is some attempt to put the OFC program in perspective with other government or foundation programs assisting minority contractors.

The original Boone-Young design for the evaluation of the Surety Bonding Program came under criticism by the Economic Innovations, Inc. Economic Innovations recommended that the design be altered so that the objectives of the program be articulated; subsequently, each alternative procedure that is designed could be tested to see how well it achieved its stated objectives. Boone-Young made some minor alterations on the design based on OFC and Economic Innovations feedback. The firm, hired under the SBA 8(a) program, has since signed a contract to do a case study evaluation of the Capital Support portion of the Banking Program.

The Future of the Opportunity
Funding Corporation
A critical variable in the funding issue is the need for early successes to satisfy OEO (which is the sole OFC funder) of OFC's worth. It appears that

two OFC–supported corporations, Wocala, Inc. and Equity Development are experiencing difficulty. Will this affect OFC's funding? Steve Nelson sheds some light on this subject:

> If the losses come fast and furious on many or all projects, we might not get refunded. The OEO people would then assume that either the concept (OFC) was wrong or that the people running it were incompetent. They would probably let the program lapse. We do not feel that much pressure for performance, though.
>
> If say during a five-year period, we have one-half of our projects successful, get a "reasonable" turnover of our funds and demonstrate realistic leverage (e.g., 10:1), we will be all right.

According to one of the authors (Doctors):

> There is also the problem of acceptability in the business community. Business leaders expect short-term performance and their natural skepticism of federal programs will be reinforced if OFC doesn't do well and *fast*.

Carol Khosrovi adds:

> If all their programs failed, we probably would not refund them. But other than that extreme, the goal is not to make any specific project a success, but is the acquisition of social knowledge.

The Board of Directors has a similar perspective to the OEO orientation. According to John Mabie:

> OFC has got to lose money. We are in a risky business, minority economic development. If, in five years, we don't fail, then we are not making risky enough deals. We expect to fail sometimes. If we don't, then the Board and the management group are not being risky enough.

And David Hertz adds:

> It is a mistake to make too much of the success or failure of a particular project, since the purpose of OFC is not to find out whether "projects" will be successful but, whether, under given circumstances, risk-sharing will loosen up and provide leverage for additional sources of capital.

> Through the end of 1972, OFC had used $300,000 of its adminis-

trative budget; this came from the $3.5 million in R & D funds, so that $7.1 million in venture funds remains. Williams explains, "We have just refunded OFC $678,000 out of Section 232 funds for administrative expenses only; no new venture funds have been awarded."

Increased funding appears to be more of a problem. According to Jack Gloster:

OFC's perception of their funding level is as follows:

> Five programs is small in the outside world's perception since they see us as an operational agency. I have not felt pressure on renewal of the grant, but for more funding; it's a problem. The $7.4 million is only good for one more program and that's it . . . $5.7 million has already been allocated to approved programs, leaving $1.3 million or so for one more program . . . probably the Consumer Credit Program.
>
> One reason we haven't implemented Opportunity Bonds yet is because it takes too much money investment. Analysts tell us you need a $3 to $5 million issue to attract market attention. So, our *creativity* is limited by our initial capitalization.

Yet, according to Willie Williams, OEO has the following perception:

> $7 million is not undercapitalized with the use of leverage. Jack has assigned $2 million to Flexible Guarantee. If he can generate 10:1 leverage, that's $20 million right there.

In sum, it has been very difficult for the OFC management to convince OEO of the need for more money. Again, this difference of opinion is a direct reflection of the difference in the two organizations' perception of OFC's role. OFC wants more money so that its programs can produce a national impact, and for that goal, more funding is surely needed. On the other hand, OEO wants experiments that are replicable; for this goal, the $7.1 million is sufficient to impact in a limited geographical area.

The CDC Problem

The CDCs have yet to be won over to the OFC camp. One of the problems is that the CDCs misunderstand OFC's role; they see OFC as merely a funding source for them. OFC plans to correct this problem by meeting with CDC directors. In addition, Williams invites EDD personnel to OFC Board of Directors meetings and gives periodic briefings to CDC people on OFC's activities. All of this represents a concerted effort on the part of Williams and the OFC management to alleviate the bad feelings between the CDC hierarchy and OFC.

The Definition of Demonstration

OEO is convinced that OFC has yet to understand the meaning of demonstration. Carol Khosrovi explains:

> The OFC staff still doesn't know what OEO means by demonstration. This will slow them down even more when they do understand, I'm afraid. Designing an experimentation/demonstration program is tough. Their proposals have always been submitted in an unacceptable form. The problem is a misunderstanding of OEO intent by OFC. OEO is not worried about losing money. The only criterion is a tight R & D design. It doesn't really matter if the project succeeds or not; if you *learn* something, that's what is so important.

Despite this indictment of OFC, she continues:

> We are not in the business of helping poor people. We are trying to find out what *does* and what *doesn't* help them. However, I am not sure that social research can be done at all, much less in a government agency. OEO is the leader in social research even as bad as we are. The state of the art is extremely low.

Measurement of Results

OFC's efforts are hidden in the wake of other, more massive programs, such as the recent $100 million public-private bank deposit program initiated by the President's Council on Minority Business Enterprises in September 1971. It is practically impossible to separate out the OFC contribution, especially since neither of the programs is being rigorously evaluated. Also, there are other difficulties. Williams states:

> . . . some OFC programs take ten years to evaluate. . . . We realize that economic development is a long-term process. . . . There are at least three years before benefits accrue in business. Economic development is a new business. It is a long hard road and immediate results are not forthcoming. For something as complex as leveraging capital, you need to operate for a while.

It appears that OEO has relaxed the pressure on OFC for early success and has decided to give the OFC projects a considerable amount of time to mature.

The Slow Start and Low Visibility of OFC

As a key OEO official, Carol Khosrovi tries to analyze the reasons for OFC's apparent slow start in getting programs underway and producing results:

A lot of people who were interested in OFC are frustrated because
of their slow start. But maybe this will mean that they will be more
effective once they do get underway. At least I hope so.

I remember talking to David Hertz at a Board meeting last year
and he too was disappointed that things hadn't moved quicker.

What we are asking them [OFC] to do is not easy. I've asked
myself, do we have the right to require such tight R & D from them
when we have our own problems in that area? We've loosened up
some.

Jack Gloster attempts to explain the underlying causes for OFC's slow start and
poor visibility to date:

There are several factors that play into OFC's low visibility and
slow start:

1. CDCs look upon OFC as a funding resource for themselves; other groups
    have this perception and this affects their perception of OFC performance.
2. The slowness of OFC in getting off the ground—fourteen months passed
    before we opened one program; six months before I even came on board,
    then eight months passed before OEO approved a program. The Real Estate
    and Flexible Guarantee Programs will have a better demonstration potential
    with better impact.
3. There have been limitations on what we have been able to achieve, e.g.,
    banking programs for liquidity enhancement. The market conditions are
    such that banks don't need liquidity. This has delayed the secondary market
    implementation.

A metaphor might be that OFC is an "eight cylinder car hitting on
two cylinders." We only had two programs approved until November
1971, then LDC was approved. It is frustrating for us.

PR–wise, we suffer from doing a limited number of projects and
our impact results are non-statistical; to evaluate OFC quantitatively
is a mistake. People evaluate OFC in terms of *operational programs*
but we are too small scale and under-funded, even for demonstration.

We have been perhaps too cautious in program implementation.
Our programs are high-risk and we have been super-cautious about
conditions under which they are implemented, e.g., we haven't
implemented the Flexible Guarantee and Real Estate programs
because the guidelines are incomplete—we designed an internal
processing system for the programs. We need to be able to respond
to peoples' needs quickly. We want to be fully "tooled up" before
we start. The program will start incrementally, not in a sudden
spurt. It will be slow getting off the ground. The central question is
in terms of visibility in community and this is still a problem. Our

emphasis: to try to do quality work and not to capitulate to pressure. However, this slow and sure technique negatively affects visibility. In historical perspective, we'll look better than we do now.

For example, there were two black contractors in Louisiana who were involved in street paving. They couldn't get bid bonds but they got performance bonds through our guarantee. It was a $350,000 guarantee; they made the low bid. Anyway, the white contractors took them to court because of no bid bond and won. The indirect effect was *good* because the black contractors got twice as much bonding as the previous quarter and double in next quarter—$1.5 million in a six-month period. Our presence gave the black contractors publicity. Also, look at the Unity case. The FDIC was brought in by OFC to protect banks *before* they go under, i.e., a new role for FDIC. Before, they would just merge them with another institution but that wouldn't work in the Unity case; a black bank can't lose its identity in this day and age.

However, we can't talk about these things because FDIC would get mad. So, again, here's a good thing we did which gets no publicity.

NOTES

1. For a full discussion of the political conceptual framework for process research, see Robert S. Weiss and Martin Rein, "The Evaluation of Broad-Aim Programs: Difficulties in Experimental Design and An Alternative," in C.H. Weiss (ed.), *Evaluating Action Programs* (Boston: Allyn and Bacon, 1972), p. 246.
2. Opportunity Funding Corporation, *Case Studies and First Year Findings of OFC's Banking and Contractor Bonding Programs* (Washington, D.C.: Opportunity Funding Corporation, 1972), p. 2.
3. Statement by Reverend Douglas Moore of Washington's United Black Front in Samuel I. Doctors and Sharon Lockwood, "Opportunity Funding Corporation: An Analysis," *Journal of Law and Contemporary Problems* (Winter 1972).
4. Theodore Cross, *Black Capitalism* (New York: Atheneum Books, 1969), p. 79.
5. Opportunity Funding Corporation, *Case Studies and First Year Findings of OFC's Banking and Contractor Bonding Programs,* pp. 2-3.
6. Don Lowitz contradicts Brazzel's statement: "I do not think that is correct, nor do I know who OEO is. OEO is many things, a number of concepts, programs and goals. I do not think it accurate to say that OFC was an alien notion to OEO. OEO under Rumsfeld was looking for various means of alleviating poverty. We were dedicated to testing as many potential projects as possible, provided they had merit. I do not see anything in OFC that is alien or in conflict with the

goals of OEO. Rumsfeld was eager to try OFC and he put a great
deal of thought into the project. It is not correct to say that there
was a conflict between OEO and OFC or that OFC was alien to
OEO at least not at the policy-making level."

7. For a complete explanation of OFC's philosophy on leverage, see Oppor-
tunity Funding Corporation, *Measuring Financial Leverage of
Indirect Financing Techniques* (Washington, D.C.: Opportunity
Funding Corporation, 1972), pp. 10–16.

8. There is a legal question involved here. *Regulation Q* of the Federal Reserve
System states the Federal Reserve Board has the right to set maximum interest rates for savings accounts at participating banks;
offering an interest subsidy may therefore be illegal. OFC is exploring this problem before implementing the program.

9. Opportunity Funding Corporation, *Case Studies and First Year Findings of
OFC's Banking and Contractor Bonding Programs,* pp. 25–26.

10. As finally approved by its Investment Committee, CAF's stock purchase
agreement incorporated an innovative plan for the eventual transfer
of CAF's shares to the employees of the bank through an employee
stock bonus trust plan.

11. This program, recommended by the President's Advisory Council on
Minority Business Enterprise and supported by the President and
the Secretary of Commerce, was to encourage deposits in minority
banks. The program has been oversubscribed by more than $100
million.

Chapter Six

Analysis of the OFC Case:
Conclusions and Recommendations

The purpose of this chapter is to analyze, with the aid of schematic sociometric charts and the use of a modified attribution analysis, the major actors and their behaviors with regard to the evaluation issue in the OFC case. This analysis will be useful in identifying those people who cluster together either in attitude or action with regard to evaluation. The purpose is to illuminate the actors' predispositions and biases, thereby projecting how these impinge on the evaluation environment and create distroted or altered images of events at a given time. This analysis does not purport to indict any individuals or organizations for their behavior on the evaluation issue; the hope is to isolate those environmental variables and circumstances that impact on the evaluation environment and impede the process of objective evaluation research. It is hoped that this analysis will help to develop a better understanding of how people within bureaucracies react to the evaluation of a social action program, and thus be helpful in anticipating problems in future evaluation settings.

The analysis begins with the sociometric chart of the evaluation environment, both in Project X days and in the current OFC/OEO situation. With this understanding of how major actors relate to each other, a model derived from attribution theory is then used to examine the changes in, or stability of, ten entities that relate to the evaluation question. Ideally, the entities should be studied in the manner in which they are viewed as various people at different times and in different situations. In the OFC case, the only time modality dimension accurately obtainable is the somewhat artificial "date of interview".

Next, the analysis proceeds with a review of salient features from the third chapter.

The Politics of Evaluation, as it relates to the OFC case. The major conclusions from the case study are delineated. In addition, the propositions outlined in Chapter One are reviewed in light of the OFC case experience. Finally, based on the preceding analysis, an attempt is made to derive techniques that might improve the research situation in a social agency setting.

Figure 6-1 is the schematic sociometric chart for "Project X" days, and Figure 6-2 illustrates the current OFC alignment. To review the role of the participants, as discussed in Chapter Five, and charted in Figures 6-1 and 6-2, the "Project X" arrangement saw Nixon appointee Donald Rumsfeld, then head of OEO, as a direct link to the president. Assisted by Dick Cheney, Rumsfeld communicated directly with Ted Cross, head of the "Project X" group, Carol Khosrovi, head of the Office of Program Development (OPD), and Geoffrey Faux, then head of the Economic Development Division (EDD). Cross, advised by Sam Doctors and assisted by Victor Sparrow, Paul London, and Dick Ramsden (with secretarial support from Devra Bloom), was the focal point for "Project X" activity. Bob Bicks, an attorney, also worked with Cross. Cross proceeded to alienate such key Congressional figures as Senators Jacob Javits and Gaylord Nelson by his request for Title ID funding.

A major conflict developed between Cross and Mike Brazzel of OEO Evaluations as to who should control the experiments of the soon-to-be-created OFC. Brazzel, Tony Partridge, and Don Lowitz, both of OEO's Legal Division, met frequently with Cross and Bicks to construct an OFC Statement of Work. Conflict developed as to OFC's autonomy and over the question of who had review authority over OFC experiments. Geoffrey Faux and his CDC-oriented Economic Development Division (EDD) were screened out by the Cross group, and they received only infrequent communications from Khosrovi and Rumsfeld.

The current OFC environment is markedly different. In the "Project X" days, the evaluation question was central to the agreement which OFC and OEO ultimately subscribed to, and its resolution took place primarily because Cross and the OEO people achieved consensus. Jack Gloster, head of OFC, has now replaced Cross as the focal point in the evaluation environment. Gloster maintains liaison with OEO through Willie Williams, head of the Business Analysis Section, OPD. Williams is now the conduit through which OFC/OEO communications pass. Boone-Young Associates, the evaluating firm, reports mainly to OEO evaluators Mike Brazzel and Hank Goldman who maintain a liaison with Williams. In addition, Boone-Young sends Williams informational copies of all findings regarding evaluation of OFC programs.

Recall from Chapter One that our intent was to use the sociometric data to construct a social space within which the power and influence processes took place. Figures 6-1 and 6-2 define that space. Figure 6-3 associates respondent attitudes and influence with that space. The figure is supplemented by Tables 6-1 and 6-2 and with a narrative to assist the reader. This presentation

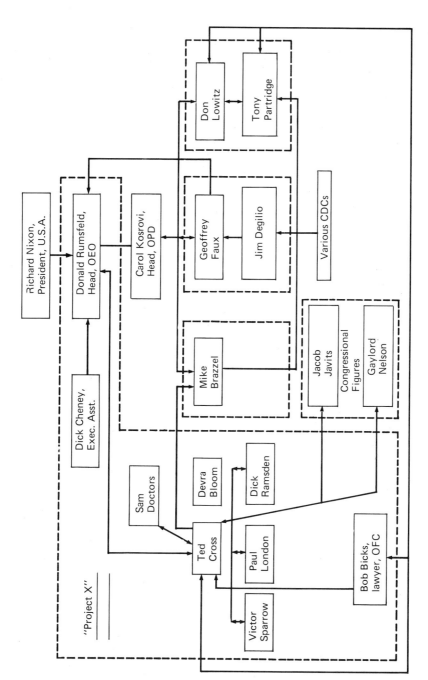

Figure 6–1. "Project X" — Sociometric Based Social Space

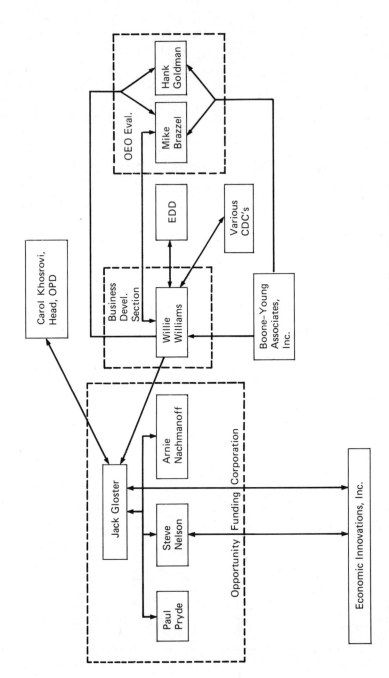

Figure 6–2. Opportunity Funding Corporation — Sociometric Based Social Space

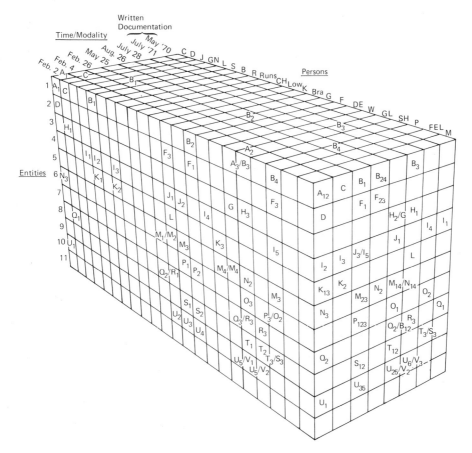

Figure 6–3. Application of Attitudes with Positions in Social Space

condenses the orientation of all major actors in one place and compares them over time. The subscripts are intended as an additional aid in locating the respondent, date of response, and nature of response. As indicated in the methodological discussion of Chapter Five, these responses are biased by such factors as selective retention, failure of memory, and rationalization.

The first entity (Entity No. 1) or attitude topic is the *nature of the role of the OFC.* Ted Cross (February 2, 1972) felt that OFC was an operational program. Likewise, Jack Gloster, on the same day, dwelt upon the operational aspects of this program. Paul London, Hank Goldman, Tony Partridge, and later on, Gloster, all stated that they felt OFC was an experimentation/demonstration program. On February 4, Jim DeGilio, a CDC supporter, felt that OFC's proper role was as a conduit for OEO resources. Entity No. 2, *feelings about the appropriateness of evaluation in a social action program,* received a "not important"

Table 6-1.   List of Major Actors in the Evaluation Environment

C   - Ted Cross, Creator of *Black Capitalism* concept and head of "Project X";

D   - Sam Doctors, Northwestern University professor who was consultant to OEO attached to "Project X";

J   - Jacob Javits, U.S. senator;

GN   - Gaylord Nelson, U.S. senator;

L   - Paul London, aide to Ted Cross on "Project X", research assistant working out of NYC;

S   - Victor Sparrow, aide to Ted Cross on "Project X", assigned to Cross by Rumsfeld, a White House fellow;

B   - Devra Bloom, secretary assigned to Cross from OEO for "Project X";

R   - Dick Ramsden, White House fellow, Rumsfeld aide;

RUM- Donald Rumsfeld, former OEO director, "Project X" days;

CH   - Dick Cheney, aide to Rumsfeld at OEO;

LOW- Don Lowitz, OEO general counsel, worked out OFC design;

K   - Carol Khosrovi, head of Office of Program Development (OPD), OEO;

Bra - Mike Brazzel, member of OFC evaluation team at OEO;

G   - Hank Goldman, member of OFC evaluation team at OEO;

F   - Geoffrey Faux, developer of CDC concept, former head of Economic Development Branch (EDD) at OEO;

De   - Jim DeGilio, leading member of EDD during "Project X" days;

W   - Willie Williams, OEO liaison to OFC;

GL   - Jack Gloster, President of OFC;

SN   - Steve Nelson, Vice President of Research and Evaluation, OFC;

P   - Tony Partridge, deputy general counsel, OEO, "Project X" days;

Fel - Marvin Feldman, OPD director before Khosrovi, saw early "Project X";

M   - John Maybie, member, OFC Board of Directors.

---

rating from Ted Cross on February 2, 1972, and an "important" designation from Hank Goldman on February 26, from Carol Khosrovi on May 25, and from Tony Partridge on May 25. As one might expect, Cross represented the "operational" orientation of OFC while Goldman, Khosrovi, and Partridge opted for evaluation. Entity No. 3, *adequateness of $7.4 million in funding toward achieving OFC's goals,* was cited as "not adequate" by Jack Gloster on May 26 and by Sam Doctors on July 28; however, on May 26, Willie Williams argued that considering OFC's leverage potential, the $7.4 million was adequate funding.

Next Entity No. 4, *purposiveness of CDC's attack on OFC,* relates to perceptions concerning hostile motives imputed to OFC's actions in acquiring Title ID funding for themselves. Senator Gaylord Nelson (April 1970), Paul London (February 2, 1972), Devra Bloom (February 4, 1972), Geoffrey Faux (Spring, 1971), and Tony Partridge (February 26, 1972) all concurred in viewing

Table 6-2. List of Major Entities and Effects

Entity No. 1. Nature of the Role of the Opportunity Funding Corp.
A - an operational program
B - an experimentation/demonstration program
C - a conduit for OEO resources

Entity No. 2. Feelings about Appropriateness of Evaluation in a Social Action Program
D - not important
E - indifferent
F - important

Entity No. 3. Adequateness of $7.4 million in Funding for Achieving OFC's Goals in Funding
G - adequate
H - not adequate

Entity No. 4. Purposiveness of OFC's attack on CDC's
I - hostile
J - not hostile

Entity No. 5. Impact of CDC Lobbying on OFC Funding
K - high
L - low

Entity No. 6. Concept of OFC's Function (Goal Clarity)
M - vehicle for testing incentives
N - OFC prototype of inst. to assist minority business

Entity No. 7. Role of OEO with Regard to OFC
O - grant maximum autonomy to do experiment
P - exercise control and review authority over experiment

Entity No. 8. Emphasis on Early OFC Success Models
Q - high
R - low

Entity No. 9. Problems with the Design of the Experiments
S - poorly written, not replicable, changed design
T - slow approval, "nit picking"

Entity No. 10. OFC Strategy for Implementing Programs
U - impact in one area/demonstration
V - nationwide visibility

OFC's action as hostile toward the CDC concept, either as an agent for Rumsfeld (who was felt to be anti-CDC) or an independent entity. On the other hand, on May 26, 1972, Carol Khosrovi and Mike Brazzel (February 26, 1972) both felt that OFC was not hostile to the CDCs. They felt that this was the only funding available to OFC and that neither Cross nor Rumsfeld had any hostile motives in seeking to acquire it. Don Lowitz, on November 17, 1972, also articulated this feeling.

Entity No. 5, *impact of CDC lobbying on OFC funding,* showed an interesting dichotomy. Paul London (February 2, 1972), Devra Bloom (February 4, 1972), and Jim Degilio (February 2, 1972) all felt that CDC lobbying was a "moral" victory over OFC because they had succeeded in reducing their funding from $20–25 million down to $7.4 million (and only $3.9 million from Title ID funds). However, on May 26, 1972, Carol Khosrovi felt that Rumsfeld had gotten all he wanted for OFC; she believed that the CDCs were fooling themselves into thinking that they had "won" over OFC. Don Lowitz (November 17, 1972) substantiated this feeling. Lowitz added that he (as Rumsfeld's aide) was surprised at the CDC opposition to OFC; he claimed that he never viewed OFC as a competitor to the CDCs.

Entity No. 6, *the concept of OFC's function,* also presents a divergence of opinion that had crystallized in early 1972. Tony Partridge and Mike Brazzel, both on February 26, 1972, concurred that while both options were discussed during the "Project X" days, OFC's role was settled (more or less) as a vehicle for testing incentives. Gloster (May 25, 1972) and Cross (February 2, 1972) saw OFC as a prototype of a firm to assist minority business. Khosrovi, in an interview (May 26, 1972) felt that *both* models were appropriate for OFC. This uncertainty about OFC's role is further demonstrated by Willie Williams who stated (May 26, 1972) that OFC was to evaluate itself as a prototype while OEO would continue to evaluate the programs. A July 12, 1972 memorandum by Louis Ramirez, director of EDD, to Jack Gloster, further confuses the issue. Ramirez requests that OFC do a semi-annual *self-evaluation* of OFC as a prototype to aid minority business and as a vehicle to implement programs.

By pointing up this role confusion to various members of the OFC staff, the researchers apparently caused OFC to clarify its goals, as the theory in Chapter Three would suggest. As noted in Chapter Five, an OFC publication states: "OFC programs and projects are selected for their potential for demonstrating successful and innovative applications of these techniques *and* for their likely impact upon the economic development of low-income communities."[1] In other words, a compromise goal position has been articulated, one which blends the evaluation-conscious OEO emphasis with the impact or operational orientation of OFC. On November 17, 1972, Don Lowitz wrote that OEO was "primarily interested in *testing* a model project which we hoped would have a *financial impact* on the poor community." It would seem that even OEO wanted OFC to have impact on the poor community, but not at the expense of a rigorous evaluation. There seemed to be a consensus at OEO that unless OFC could be constrained in its "deal making," the results of its operations would not be able to be evaluated.

Entity No. 7, *the role of OEO with regard to OFC,* also was a source of differing perceptions. Mike Brazzel, Hank Goldman, and Tony Partridge (February 26, 1972) concurred separately that OEO needed to exercise firm control over all programs. Partridge, in a memorandum of July 21, 1971, also added that OFC needed "maximum autonomy" to conduct programs. On May 26, 1972, Gloster also saw a need for OFC to maintain autonomy over all its programs. These two stances are obviously a source of perpetual conflict between OFC and OEO. Lowitz, however, felt that the conflicts were resolved in the OFC grant and that everything was compatible.

Perceptions of the *OEO emphasis on early OFC success models* (Entity No. 8) show some interesting changes. Sam Doctors, in a memorandum written for Ted Cross in May 1970, expressed a high degree of concern for early success models; Jack Gloster, in an interview (February 2, 1972), concurred in this strategy. Carol Khosrovi revealed in an interview (May 26, 1972) that early in the OFC/OEO relationship, OEO might have pressured OFC too much in terms of evaluation pressure and need-for-success pressure; however, she added that the pressure in both areas was much relaxed now. Steve Nelson in a telephone interview (July 28, 1972) confirmed this analysis.

Entity No. 9, *problems with the design of the experiments,* produces a rather predictable dichotomy. Hank Goldman and Mike Brazzel, on February 26, 1972, agreed that the proposals were poorly written, hard to understand, and made assumptions that were not clear. They viewed this as a direct threat to the experimental design in terms of reliable and valid results. They also claimed that OFC changed the Surety Bonding design after the criteria for evaluation had been settled upon in joint OFC/OEO meetings, thereby jeopardizing the design. To Jack Gloster and Steve Nelson (May 26, 1972), the main problem was OEO's intransigence in approving the designs and their criticisms of OFC-submitted proposals. Tony Partridge, in a memorandum (July 21, 1971), allowed that OEO had been "unconscionably slow" in approving OFC designs and chastized OFC for not worrying enough about whether the proposals would produce good, replicable experiments.

The final entity in the social space analysis, perceptions about the *OFC strategy for implementing programs* (Entity No. 10) again illustrates lack of consensus, even among the two "sides" of the issue. On February 2, 1972, Ted Cross felt that the program should be concentrated in one area, but *not* for demonstration purposes, since he felt the techniques did not need to be evaluated. Rather, he wanted to produce the "financial synergy" of *Black Capitalism,* wherein many financial incentives impinge on the same geographic area and same institutions to produce synergistic results. Therefore, Cross was an unwitting ally to the evaluation-conscious OEO people who wanted to demonstrate the incentives in a limited geographical area. Such sentiments were expressed by Hank Goldman and Mike Brazzel (February 26, 1972) and Steve Nelson (July 28, 1972); however, they also expressed a need to increase OFC's visibility at the national level. Therein lies a basic problem: with limited funding of $7.4 million, it is difficult to have national impact on minority enterprise for maximum visibility and to do a demonstration experiment at the same time. The limited funding requires a limited geographical area for demonstration, yet pressures for visibility force OFC to spread its resources nationwide. John Mabie believes that OFC has achieved both goals of demonstration and national visibility. He mentioned that possible SBA changes in the 90 percent guarantees and the FDIC policy change in the Unity Bank case could have national impact.

REVIEW OF THE POLITICS OF EVALUATION
AS APPLIED TO THE CASE STUDY

The first and foremost problem of *The Politics of Evaluation* is the conflict between those who operate the programs (and believe in them) and those who analyze the programs (whose job it is to be skeptical of them).[2] In the OFC, this conflict existed, but not in the classic sense. The conflict has been between OFC and OEO, which hired the evaluators. This hostility occurred for at least two reasons: (1) in OFC's eyes, OEO is the evaluator even though it is not physically carrying out the evaluation process: OFC is dependent on OEO for funding, and this further intensifies OFC's anxiety with regard to OEO's evaluation function: and (2) the original CDC/OFC funding conflict never has been totally resolved; there are those people at OEO (in EDD) who still hold much animosity against OFC because of what they regard as "stolen" Title ID funds.

The program administrator, when he is the "trapped administrator," (see Chapter 3, pp. III–37 to III–39 for a discussion of this concept) must of necessity be a program advocate. Both Ted Cross, in the original "Project X" days, and subsequently Jack Gloster, are strong OFC program advocates. Especially with Cross, techniques were advocated as though they were certain to be successful. Such an orientation leads to either an indifference or an open hostility toward evaluation; it is safe to conclude that in both Cross and Gloster's case, indifference would be more likely. Cross stated emphatically that since the incentives he was recommending had been tested within a variety of socioeconomic contexts, they were bound to work in a ghetto environment. In *Black Capitalism,* Cross compares the ghetto or barrio environment to that of a so-called underdeveloped country. Related to this orientation is the implicit assumption among implementers or program administrators that effective full-scale programs can be launched which can significantly improve the lives of the poor.[3] Ted Cross and, to a certain degree, Jack Gloster and Steve Nelson, all see OFC as the forerunner of a large, well-funded national minority funding program. Cross views OFC as a necessary step to prove what he already knows to be true in order that a powerful national corporation can be funded. In other words, OFC is only a formality designed to satisfy the funding agency (OEO), potential funding sources, and Congress that the theory of *Black Capitalism* is viable. OFC does not demonstrate a strong interest in determining which variables determine success or failure in a program through a rigorous experimental design; rather, the emphasis at OEO and OFC now is on the case study approach.[4] This can be interpreted as an admission by OEO that rigorous experimental designs are impossible to implement in the social agency setting; Carol Khosrovi also has voiced serious doubts about such an approach.

The impact of negative findings traditionally produces strong political ramifications in the social agency setting. In the early OFC days (1970-71), OEO placed rigorous evaluation restrictions on OFC proposal designs; many meetings were held with OEO evaluation staff and OFC management to produce experiment-oriented proposals. Then, OEO relaxed the pressure. Willie Williams notes that "economic development takes a long time to show results," so the pressure for immediate success was "unrealistic." Carol Khosrovi states that "we can't expect OFC to be perfect when we have so many problems ourselves." It thus appears that rigorous evaluation research is out of the picture as an active variable in the OEO/OFC relationship. And Steve Nelson, OFC Vice President for Research and Evaluation, states that "We will get refunded unless all of our projects fail."

There are some non-political barriers to evaluation research at OFC. Administrators resent the intrusion of outside evaluators. Jack Gloster expressed apprehension about the study presented in this book. Gloster feared that this research would use up time that the OFC staff could use more profitably tackling operation problems. Gloster has little confidence in the use of the scientific method and, in a letter to one of the authors, he "hopes your efforts will produce more than just another research paper."

Extensive political barriers at OFC exist against evaluation research. As stated earlier, the public availability of scientific evidence which may attest to the failure of a program reduces the privacy and security of administrators. Gloster has stated a need for OFC to become "visible," but by that he meant that more OFC successes should become evident. The possibility of a negative evaluation outcome is not the type of visibility an administrator desires. With the "positive visibility" criterion in mind, Gloster is concerned with the reactive effects of this research. He fears that this research might give away information that will jeopardize OFC's politically tenuous situation. OFC's many potential detractors are eager to use negative information on OFC against the Corporation. Agency administrators are typically apprehensive about "snoopers" in their bailiwick. Early in this research, Steve Nelson refused access to OFC files, presumably because of the potential compromise of private OFC information.

Supra-agency people often are uptight about innovative programs and therefore prejudge them negatively. According to Mike Brazzel, this is what happened at OEO with the OFC project. Evaluation is thus used as a political tool to eliminate the threatening program. Said Brazzel, "The EDD people, who supported the CDC concept, wanted to evaluate OFC in the hopes that they [OFC] would look bad; evaluation is the 'hatchet' man at OEO."

Since administrators often assume that their programs work, evaluations sometimes are designed to show that everything works, rather than showing that some programs work better than others. Steve Nelson appears to approach evaluation with this orientation, although he protests that "we have not made any prejudgment about the effectiveness of our techniques." More correctly, it is not Nelson's job to insure that discriminating evaluative designs are implemented; this is ultimately OEO's (and Boone-Young's) responsibility. Regardless of this, administrators, because of their vested interests in the program, are socialized into taking the success of programs for granted even if they themselves were not involved in the program's design. OFC would appear to follow this norm.

Administrators often are concerned that evaluations are not really scientific and cannot be relied upon to produce valid and reliable results. Gloster has shown his contempt for the "typical" social science research in which very little aid is forthcoming for the subject(s) of the research. Administrators have had bad experiences with social science researchers in the past; these researchers come in, ask a few embarrassing questions, then leave, and totally fail to help solve the problems that they purported to study. Gloster has expressed the hope that this research will be helpful in improving OFC's effectiveness. The authors certainly adhere to this goal.

An inherent conflict often exists between the policy level (OEO) and the operations level (OFC) in a social action setting. Evaluations usually are supported by the policy people who must face questions regarding the allocation of resources; this is especially true of OEO, which has been a politically volatile program since its inception. OEO, like other large federal agencies, is staffed with bureaucrats who operate in the bureaucratic reward system which creates tremendous insecurity. Under this system

> the rewards for accomplishment are much less than the penalties for failure. . . . For the bureaucrat, avoiding political embarrassment rather than accomplishing program goals is the first priority.[5]

Therefore, policy-level bureaucrats typically want proof of the efficacy of their decisions; evaluation oftentimes can provide this "proof." However, policy-makers often are unable to enforce conditions that are essential for sound, empirical research upon their operating units. OEO tried for a while, but it has apparently concluded that prospects were dim for conducting the type of social research originally planned for OFC experiments.

At the operations level, organization members also are concerned with avoiding political embarrassment. Moreover, the operations level (OFC) has the most to lose from a negative evaluation.

Originally, programs goals were unclear at OFC. This resulted from the unresolved issue regarding the role of OFC. The overt role of OFC (that being measured by Boone-Young using related goal criteria) is that of an experimental/demonstration program. However, a strong covert role orientation apparently consists of getting money into strategic minority businesses to improve their viability, thereby promoting minority economic development. This role is not being considered in the OEO-directed Boone-Young evaluation, and therefore any positive movement in this direction by OFC will escape measurement.

Program changes also raise problems in the OEO/OFC relationship. One OEO official complained that OFC kept changing the Surety Bonding design after the experiment supposedly was agreed upon and formalized. Changes in the program can make an evaluation design obsolete; if the experimenters persist in the original measures, they will evaluate the wrong criteria and good effects of the program will go unmeasured. This problem has been eliminated in the current OEO/OFC relationship; programs no longer will be changed by OFC after an agreement has been reached.

Typical administrative responses to evaluation include subversion of data, restricted access, and the like. With the single exception of one of the researchers having been told that OFC files were off-limits at the beginning of the project, this has not been the case at OFC. OFC officials have gone out of their way to cooperate, to approve interviews and to be always candid about OFC operations and the OEO/OFC relationship.

Review of the General Propositions in Light of Case Study

Despite the limitations in a case study approach with respect to generalizing, several propositions were generated with an eye toward testing them in a limited fashion. Each proposition is examined in light of the OFC case experience, and a statement about the case's complete or partial support of the proposition is made.

Propositions from Literature Search.

P. 1. *Historically, evaluation results have not been used in agency policymaking processes.*

The Boone-Young evaluation report was submitted to OEO in July 1973. The report was generally favorable toward the OFC bonding program.

OFC management seemed little effected by the report particularly since the report provided little new data. Thus, it is difficult to fully assess the validity of Proposition 1 in the OFC context. However, based on the behavior and predisposition of the major actors in the evaluation environment, we can make some tentative judgments in this regard. Gloster has shown some disdain for "typical research reports." The OFC evaluation posture, while not negative, can hardly be considered enthusiastic. The OEO position on evaluation definitely has softened from a hard-line, objective, rigorous orientation into a more loosely structured approach, thereby potentially reducing Boone-Young's evaluation design to a descriptive one. Given these facts, it seems unlikely that the OFC management will be significantly influenced by future evaluation results, unless OEO reapplies the evaluation pressure. On the other hand, both Gloster and Nelson had indicated that they planned to use the results of the Boone-Young evaluation as an aid to improved decision making; they still appear somewhat interested in the potential role of evaluation research in policymaking and are willing to learn about how they might fit into such a dynamic process.

P. 2.   *Evaluation research is a political tool, depending both upon the perspective and value set held by the viewer and upon whether or not the results are (or are anticipated to be) positive or negative toward the program in question.*

Early in the OFC study, we saw that OFC was designed as a "showcase" program for President Nixon's concept of minority capitalism. OFC is presently the only experimental program for ameliorative social action produced by the Nixon Administration. Thus it would stand to reason that a positive evaluation was desired by that administration. As stated earlier, evaluation has been used as a "hatchet man" at OEO; it must be concluded that many opponents of OFC (primarily CDC supporters) would welcome an early (and hopefully negative) evaluation of the OFC experiment.

Even if OFC's evaluation were negative, it is questionable whether such an outcome would have of itself influenced the policy of the Nixon Administration. It remains to be seen how the Ford administration will respond to evaluations.

P. 2.   (continued) *The principal protagonists in the politics of evaluation are the administrators (whose job it is to support and implement the program) and the evaluator (whose job it is to be critical of the program).*

The above has been supported in the OFC case. However, it should be added that Gloster has been much more receptive to evaluation than the literature on the politics of evaluation would suggest. Of course, control of the evaluation is out of his hands since OEO gave Boone-Young their direction.

P. 2. (continued) *The Political structure uses evaluation as a political tool–that is, those in power use positive evaluations to authenticate programs they support, they selectively ignore those findings which are incongruent with their beliefs, and they purposely suppress positive evaluations of programs they oppose.*

The data in this case are inconclusive with regard to this proposition. Since there has been no full-scale evaluation of OEO's programs, it is difficult to speculate on the ultimate disposition of the results. However, based on the previous discussion of the Nixon Administration and its support for the prevailing free enterprise system, one might project that, even if the evaluation were to prove negative, it would not have resulted in dissolution of OFC.

P. 3. *Vague or diffuse goal formulation can be a direct result of the politics of evaluation.*

The OFC case bears out this proposition. In the pre-OFC days, OEO members such as Partridge, Lowitz, Brazzel, and Rumsfeld met with Cross and his staff to work out a compromise on the role of evaluation at OFC. The issue was never fully resolved. As a result, the goals of OFC were not rigorously articulated. Instead, each program's goals were considered independently as OEO evaluated the OFC program proposals. OFC now has clarified its goals.

P. 3. (continued) *In the presence of vague or diffuse goals, perceptions by different actors in different bureaucratic levels concerning the role of a given social agency color their orientation toward evaluation of that agency's programs.*

As documented, OEO personnel uniformly see OFC as an experimentation/demonstration program and, as such, have a strong positive feeling about the need for evaluation (even though the emphasis has diminished from "Project X" days). OFC personnel and the "Project X" people (especially Cross) view OFC in more of an operational vein and see evaluation as a nice addition, but certainly not a critical one to the success of the corporation. OFC board members are strongly pro-evaluation. According to Williams, CDC personnel have a tendency to view OFC as a conduit for their funds and, as such, they see little role for evaluation of OFC programs.

P. 4. *Evaluation research is most often supported by those policymakers whose job it is to allocate resources among competing programs.*

This proposition is supported by the research. OEO, in this case the policymaker, was in a very vulnerable political situation. It now seems evident that the Nixon Administration was hostile toward OEO and would have liked to alter its function radically or else eliminate it completely. Consequently, OEO officials have generally been required to back their funding requests for specific programs to Congress with hard data on the relative effectiveness of those programs. In this case, if OEO wishes to provide significant new funding to OFC, there will be a need for some hard analytical data from evaluations to support the funding.

P. 5.   *Many agency administrators (and/or program designers) assume that their programs work and do not see the need for evaluating a principle they already "know" to be true.*

The OFC case supports this proposition. Ted Cross is quoted as believing in his theoretical approach and as not seeing the relevance of testing techniques that we know work well in various socioeconomic contexts. Also, Gloster must be confident in the techniques as it is his job to promote them from a public relations standpoint. However, balance does exist. Through OEO's lessened pressure on evaluation, OFC can afford to fail, thereby enhancing its chances to truly explore the applicability of various approaches (at least from a qualitative, non-rigorous perspective).

P. 6.   *Because of the politics of evaluation research, the assumption that proper research leads to policy improvement is naive.*

Since the first evaluation, that of the Surety Bonding program provided little hard data. It is not possible to evaluate this proposition in the OFC context. However, there are indications that OFC is sensitive to evaluation results. In the first place, goal clarification has occurred, and is at least partially due to researchers' focus on that problem. Also, Nelson has just published some case studies of the Banking and Surety Bonding programs that include suggestions for policy changes.

P. 7.   *Social action programs often are designed with little thought as to how they can be most effective or how we can learn the most from them through quality evaluation research.*

The OFC experience tends to partially refute this proposition. There had been intense interest in evaluation with regard to OFC's program, both in the "Project X" days and after the incorporation of OFC. However, the program was designed by Ted Cross, and the case study provides ample evidence to indicate that Cross was not concerned about the evaluation of his program.

The evaluation environment at OFC is highly political and, as such, has apparently passed beyond a point at which objective, rigorous research could be accomplished. Former President Nixon wanted OFC to succeed and the CDCs wanted it to fail; the politics of this volatile environment militated against objective and thorough-going research efforts.

Propositions from Research.

P. 8. *Evaluation and operations are mutually exclusive orientations in a practical sense—that is, it would be difficult to find an aggressive, effective administrator who had a high priority on quality evaluation.*

The roles of the program administrator and the evaluator have inherent conflicting interests. The program administrator has to be the program advocate, and Jack Gloster is no exception. If an individual wishes to provide effective support for a program, he must believe it is effective in achieving its stated objectives. This orientation automatically keeps the administrator from functioning as an objective proponent of evaluation research. The only exception would be if the administrator were *so confident* that either because of the program's excellence or because of his effective control of the measurement criteria to insure good results, he surely would get a positive evaluation. Gloster certainly is not an active opponent of evaluation, as the literature on the politics of evaluation suggest, but on the other hand, he could scarcely be considered an active proponent for evaluation research. He does have a strong evaluation man in Steve Nelson, who seems to balance operational and evaluation considerations.

P. 9. *Many levels of bureaucracy are typically involved in the politics of evaluation research, each with a somewhat different perspective on the proper role for evaluation.*

As has previously been demonstrated in this research, both OFC (operating agency) and OEO (supra-agency) have been embroiled in political controversy about the evaluation of OFC's programs since "Project X" days. However, OEO's use of the evaluation issue as an important constraint on OFC activities has diminished in recent months and, therefore, evaluation's use as a political tool has lessened. In the "Project X" days, we found that some OEO people wanted to evaluate OFC's programs in the hopes they would be found wanting. The new emphasis at OEO, articulated by Williams and Khosrovi, indicates that the politicization of evaluation research will be reduced in future OFC/OEO contacts, since a more qualitative (and less rigorous) design now is deemed acceptable to OEO.

In addition to these levels of bureaucracy, the political structure itself is highly involved in the politics of evaluation. This structure has its own perception of the proper role for evaluation, depending upon its openness to change and/or its willingness to have its basic assumptions challenged in the light of close scrutiny.

P. 10.   *Evaluation research can degenerate into intense role playing with no serious commitment to evaluation research by any of the parties involved in the politics of evaluation.*

The OFC case tends to support this proposition. Early OEO enthusiasm for evaluation has dampened considerably, presumably because of the immense political and non-political barriers to effective evaluation research. Evaluation has been reduced to somewhat of a game wherein each of the parties pretends to be interested in evaluation. OEO was especially attached to this orientation, since the agency was under constant fire from the Nixon Administration and needed "support" for its policy decisions concerning the allocation of its resources. The quality of the evaluation research is somewhat secondary to the fact that *an evaluation research is being done.* OFC is less hypocritical about its orientation; it is candidly admitted that most of their interest in evaluation research results from OEO's pressures in the area. There is nothing intrinsically wrong with these orientations if they are well known to each party. The danger lies in creating the illusion of a strong emphasis on rigorous evaluation research in a social agency in which, in fact, such an emphasis does not exist.

Major Conclusions from the Case Study

There appears to be little commitment to rigorous, scientific evaluation by OFC management. Superficially, this appears to be a continuation of the orientation that originated with Ted Cross. Cross indicated that he saw no problem with refunding OFC in the absence of an evaluation. OFC does not seem to be vitally interested in evaluation, but it is naive to expect it to be since, like most social agencies, it has little to gain and much to lose. OFC's goals seem to be (1) getting money into minority communities; (2) assisting minority businesses in becoming economic units; (3) demonstrating that Cross' techniques work; (4) doing such evaluations as necessary to placate OEO; and (5) developing into a much larger, better-funded national minority funding corporation.

OEO was initially interested in evaluation in the OFC experiments. However, it is difficult to conclude just how much of this interest stemmed from a sincere commitment to rigorous evaluation and how much from the fact that OEO sees itself in a certain role and feels obligated to live up to that role. In the early days at OFC, great pressure was put on the corporation to submit rigorous, experimental proposals—the orientation seemed to be "If it can't be evaluated, it shouldn't be done." OEO's own glaring inadequacies in the evaluation research area subsequentially became evident to OEO's management; as Khosrovi suggests, it scarcely seemed fair for OEO to demand such rigor from OFC when their own house was not in order. Khosrovi expresses skepticism as to whether it is indeed possible to conduct rigorous evaluation research in a government social agency setting.

OEO's reduced pressure can be linked to the reduced role of the Northwestern University consulting group, Economic Innovations, Inc. Once OFC sensed OEO's decreased emphasis, their needs for consulting on evaluation strategy lessened. *Experimental* evaluation of OFC programs now seems to be a "dead" issue, both at OEO and OFC. Case studies have been completed for the Banking and Surety Bonding Programs, and the final Boone-Young report on the Surety Bonding Program is largely a descriptive piece. Nelson, in a memorandum (June 14, 1972) articulates an OFC policy of interim and final evaluations of OFC projects for the purpose of determining "the success or failure of individual programs . . . to provide a partial basis for recommendations."

> OFC-conducted evaluations will concentrate primarily on the factors which are most directly affected by its risk reduction and incentive techniques. These factors include capital flow to projects, employment generated by projects, direct social benefits, OFC costs, i.e., losses and project-related expenses. Because of its limited resources for conducting evaluation, OFC will not attempt the measurement of indirect benefits, e.g., the multiplier effect of economic activity in poverty areas, community social benefit, etc. Hopefully, the OEO-conducted evaluations will address these important synergistic effects of OFC projects. Wherever possible, OFC evaluations will present statistical data on such items as capital generated, sales and revenues, profitability of projects, direct employment, leverage determination, OFC costs and losses, in order to substantiate the financial techniques involved. In unique situations, where a single demonstration is significant in illustrating the effectiveness of a technique, a detailed case study will be undertaken to present the findings. In particular, on projects where losses are incurred, the case study method may be helpful in uncovering "what went wrong" and how to improve the technique used.

In this document, Nelson discusses the limitations to the evaluation of OFC experiments. He sees experiments as an impossibility since OFC must try its incentives in a market economy over which it has little control. "The conventional experimental method . . . is usually unavailable for OFC projects." In Nelson's eyes, OFC's limited funding necessitates insufficient sample replication of an experiment and/or an insufficient sample size for statistically significant results to be obtained. Finally, the "time element also has an inhibiting effect on the evaluation." An ideal evaluation would concern itself not only with the OFC involvement period, but also beyond that period. According to Nelson, "While projects that result in failure have a readily identifiable time span, there is a problem in defining the point in time when an OFC-supported project is considered a success." At best, says Nelson, arbitrary time periods can be used to establish relevant time frames for evaluation.

A memorandum from Louis Ramirez of EDD further substantiates OEO's reduced emphasis on experimental evaluation. The emphasis on self-evaluation is new at OEO. At an OFC board meeting (February 24, 1972), Jack Gloster asked OEO's Willie Williams if the 10 percent of OEO funds allocated to the evaluation of its social action programs (such as OFC) could be turned over to OFC for data collection and self-evaluation purposes. Gloster's request was refused. The above raises an important area of the evaluation question, namely, *who does the evaluation research?* As originally set up, OFC was to do a self-evaluation of its agency as a vehicle for minority economic development, and OEO was to evaluate the individual programs. It would seem that a reverse orientation would be more realistic. OFC, being closer to the source, would seem more qualified to evaluate the effectiveness of the individual techniques, while OEO would seem better suited to evaluate OFC as a prototype of an institution designed to stimulate minority business.

OFC's primary operational orientation produces other impediments to the evaluation of its programs. In the first place, OFC does not achieve the financial synergy that Cross discusses in *Black Capitalism* because "it diffuses funds by planning their expenditure in a large number of cities instead of concentrating the funds . . . which frustrates the intention of Title ID, which sought to make sufficient funds available to make a real impact in selected areas." [6] By concentrating in one area, it is much easier to show results and to demonstrate incentives. However, with OFC's previous tendency to strike while the iron is hot in making deals to help minority business people, this result can be frustrated.

Another problem relating to the evaluation issue is the question of paternalism. A major community development association publication notes:

> It is clear that the major program issue is the extent to which low-income people should organize for the economic development of their own poverty areas. To quote from Cross' book: "The solution (for enrichment of the ghetto) lies in ignoring the propaganda of black militants and in doggedly pursuing the route of clear logic and justice: the *forced* injection of credit, risk capital,

and entrepreneurial skills into the ghetto community." It is the
forced character of the Cross plan, without regard to the development of local capacities, which is seen as perhaps the most objection-
able aspect of the proposed program.[7]

Yet another problem between OEO and OFC regarding the evalua-
tion issue is the continuing misunderstanding over OFC's role. Even within
OEO, disagreement continues on this subject. Carol Khosrovi sees OFC's role as
twofold: first as a vehicle to test experiments and, second, as a prototype of an
institution to help minority business. To Mike Brazzel and Tony Partridge,
OFC's sole role is that of a vehicle to test experiments. Jack Gloster and Steve
Nelson both tend to view OFC as a prototype of a national funding corporation.
Some clarifying of OFC's role has come out of recent OFC literature, but,
essentially, these areas of differences have persisted.

With the OFC case as evidence, it becomes clear that Suchman,
Wholey, and others whose "principles of evaluation research" are articulated
above gloss over some of the more difficult issues in the substance and use
of evaluative research. Evaluations are rarely the clean, helpful pieces of social
research that these writers indicate. The assumptions regarding evaluation
research and its process of implementation, as defined in this chapter, seem
idealistic when compared with the OFC experience. Such statments as "There
is an intrinsic relationship between evaluation and program planning and development" seem to reflect more wishful thinking than actual fact. Projections
concerning evaluation as the "wave of the future" have substantive support
among leading social scientists, yet the OFC case points up strong political
factors that impede the conduct of evaluative research.

The different attitudes and perceptions of major actors in the evaluation environment cause them to be constant and antagonists, blaming each
other for supposed rigid thinking and non-cooperation. Administrators and
evaluators are not the same kind of people, and it is naive to expect them to be
able to cooperate fully with one another and to have a full appreciation for each
others' problems and perspectives. People do not understand the intent of
evaluation research in the "experimenting society,"[8] and they tend to see
the evaluation in strictly political terms.

The tragic result of all this is that, because of the bureaucratic
reward system and the insecurities that it fosters, a kind of game playing is
engendered. OEO continues to profess an interest in experimental evaluation,
and OFC argues that it is committed to the effective evaluation of its programs.
In truth, neither party seems genuinely committed to its goal. OFC seems to be
the more open of the two with regard to its view of evaluation research. That
agency's personnel seem to feel that, given all the environmental constraints
to rigorous research, the case method seems to work best.

Suggestions for the De-Politicization of the
Evaluation Environment

The foregoing is not meant to suggest the situation is totally hope-less. However, to achieve successful application of experimental evaluation designs in a social agency setting, some basic changes will have to be made in the method in which it is conducted. The following section explores some contemporary thought in this area.

With regard to the "latent conservative function" of evaluation stud-ies, the client's resistance to negative research findings presents a real political bar-rier to the improvement of social action programs through research inputs into the policy process.[9] Carter asserts that the reason that negative results have so little impact on an organization is because "the practitioners (and sometimes the researchers) never seriously entertain the possibility that the results could come out negatively or be insignificant; without commitment to the net, one or both of the gamblers usually welch(es)."[10] To alleviate this problem, Carter suggests that the researcher should confront the client with as many alternative findings as possible before he begins his study; tentative organiza-tional adaptations can thus be anticipated for each possible result.

This suggestion is a subset of a broader area, that of educating the parties to an evaluation about the problems and potentials of their relationship. Both parties to the evaluation should be educated so that they can achieve some empathy into one another's perspectives. The evaluator should be made aware of the pressures on the administrator and of his likely response to such pressures. Likewise, the administrator should be made aware of the true, non-political role of the objective evaluator. The two roles can be made some-what compatible, if not supportive of each other, through the use of mutual education.

There are several other areas in which the evaluation environment can be improved. The milieu for meaningful evaluation involves a meaningful interaction between methodology, bureaucracy, and politics. Therefore, attacks on an evaluation sometimes may be methodological in form but ideological in concern (e.g., the Head Start example discussed earlier). Since it is so difficult to structure a tight social science experiment even without the political con-siderations involved, an ideological enemy (or supporter) of a program may use the weaknesses of the design to discredit the results (or alternatively point up the "scientific" nature of the results to strengthen the program's political position). To depoliticize the evaluation and its results as much as possible, major evaluations of programs should be conducted by an office or staff that is removed from the operating situation. Objective evaluation is a very difficult task for the ego-involved manager. A separate office being charged specifically with the task of program measurement, not program defense, can at least institutionalize a degree of objectivity. Also, to hedge against a popular program (e.g., Head Start) being negatively evaluated with all the political ramifications considered thereby, there must be a concerted effort to develop new ideas for restructuring ongoing programs and developing new ones as well as for testing the merits of these approaches before large-scale programs are mounted nationally. Finally, Evans and Williams, conclude their analysis with this event:

> We recognize the danger that the results of evaluation and systematic testing can be ill-used. But what course of action is not dangerous? What 'good' approach cannot be turned to evil? Is it not more hazardous to proceed boldly as if we know when we do not?[11]

The determination of program effectiveness is a key management function. Evaluation is (or ideally should be) a central part of the decision-making process and should, therefore, be given a superordinate position within the agency. Evans and Williams contend that "The ideal type of arrangement is one which combines the key executive functions of planning, programming, evaluating, and budgeting in a single staff arm which serves as the agency director's key advisor and implementing arm."[12]

The evaluation function needs professionally qualified people as well as an invulnerable source of funds to produce quality work. If these are not present, the evaluation leaves itself open to political attack in which the methodology is impugned primarily for political reasons.

Is it possible to separate out the two factors that must be considered in designing an effective research program? On the one hand, the behavioral, political, structural, and methodological problems must be involved. For the effective conduct of evaluation research:

1. The research must address the policymaker's objectives.
2. The alternatives examined must be operationally relevant.
3. The methodology must provide valid results that are convincing to the policymaker.
4. The policymaker must receive the results in a timely, intelligible, non-threatening fashion.[13]

On the other hand, once these problems are solved, evaluation strategy still must be matched to the nature of the particular program.

The two factors that determine the nature of the program are (1) the degree of goal definition and (2) the degree of obtainable knowledge.[14] Goals, or program objectives, were discussed earlier. By degree of obtainable knowledge is meant the adequacy of the researcher's understanding of cause-effect relationships, and measurability of relevant variables. Can the researchers operationalize important program inputs and outputs? Are appropriate data available, or do researchers have substantial funds for data collection? A program with defined goals and a high degree of obtainable knowledge calls for a very different evaluation strategy than does a program with undefined goals and a low degree of obtainable knowledge. In fact, one could hypothesize that from the foregoing case analysis, programs with undefined or diffuse goals and a low degree of obtainable knowledge should opt for qualitative process research. On the other hand, programs with well-defined goals and a high degree of obtainable knowledge should be evaluated experimentally.

The notions above are attempts to develop an effective fit between types of social action programs and forms of evaluation. The central message in this case study is that evaluators who impose themselves in a federal context should learn the political lessons provided by the now numerous attempts to evaluate federal social action, and then apply those lessons to their own research. The important lessons which are apparent in the Head Start evaluations, the New Jersey negative income tax evaluations, the experience of the Opportunity Funding Corporation, and others, are not primarily statistical. Legitimate efforts are underway to develop methodological and statistical strategies which can be applied in more open and responsive bureaucratic environments. But to apply those insensitively in present day, politically charged social action settings will only exacerbate the distance and lack of cooperation among program and administrative personnel, program clients, and evaluators.

Evaluators must be sensitive to the political realities which shape the form and substance of federal social action, while simultaneously seeking to sensitize program personnel and program clients to ways in which their cooperation might enhance the utility of the research for them and for the program. In addition, they must recognize when the interests of administrative personnel and program clients clash, and when evaluations serve neither. Where administrators should learn to appreciate sensitive evaluation efforts, evaluators must learn to take a new stance toward administrative decisions which undercut the potential for pure research. In the present state of the art there is more to be gained by considering solutions to such events when they occur than by bemoaning the fate of any particular evaluation.

Given our present knowledge, fully documented qualitative studies often transcend the utility of thoroughly quantitative approaches, for one cannot now quantify the powerful political influences on evaluation. The evaluator must be acutely aware of the methods one would apply in an optimum research situation, and must learn as well to cooperate with agency personnel and clients in developing that mix of rigor and flexibility which will achieve the most that can be learned in any particular social action context.

NOTES

1. Opportunity Funding Corporation, *Case Studies and First-Year Findings of OFC's Banking and Contractor Bonding Programs* (Washington, D.C.: Opportunity Funding Corporation, 1972), pp. 2–3.

2. John W. Evans and Walter Williams, "The Politics of Evaluation: The Case of Head Start," *The Annals of the American Academy of Political and Social Science* (September 1969), pp. 118–32.

3. Theodore Cross, *Black Capitalism* (New York: Atheneum, 1969).

4. Since the "traumatic" Surety Bonding experience, OEO has shown a preference for the more qualitative case study approach. The Capital Support program is being analyzed in this fashion. Also, Steve Nelson of OFC has indicated that he recommends the use of the case study approach in ascertaining what such projects as Equity Development, Ogala Sioux, and Wocala, Inc., have experienced as difficulties. In fact, David Hertz, in a letter to David K. Banner, August 22, 1972, gave the following description of the problems encountered in social evaluation, indicating a need for a more sober, perhaps qualitative view: "As to the issue of evaluation, this has been a problem for all demonstration projects that relate to economic matters. For example, I believe that OEO is in no position to 'evaluate' the effectiveness of the CDCs themselves in economic terms. I and most of our Board members have had close relstionships with one or another CDC over the years, and I think we know something about the difficulty of measuring their economic impact. It is entirely possible that one effective demonstration capital encouragement situation is sufficient to indicate replicability. It is possible also that 100 such situations could demonstrate nothing except individual idiosyncratic viewpoints in local communities."

5. Geoffrey Faux, "Politics and Bureaucracy in Community-Controlled Economic Development," *Law and Contemporary Problems* (Spring 1971), p. 278.

6. Draft Position Paper of the National Economic Development Congress, Washington, D.C., April 20, 1970, pp. 2–3.

7. "News from NACD," a publication of the National Association for Community Development, Washington, D.C., April 10, 1970, p. 1.

8. See Donald T. Campbell, "Methods for the Experimenting Society," unpublished manuscript, Northwestern University, 1972.

9. Reginald K. Carter, "Client's Resistance to Negative Findings and the Latent Conservative Function of Evaluation Studies," *The American Sociologist* (May 1971), pp. 118–124.

10. Ibid., p. 123.

11. Evans and Williams, "The Politics of Evaluation," p. 132.

12. Ibid., pp. 118–132.

13. Noralou P. Roos, "Evaluation, Quasi-Experimentation and Public Policy: Observations by a Short Term Bureaucrat," in J.A. Caporaso and L.L. Roos, Jr. (eds.), *Quasi-Experimenta: Testing Theory and Evaluating Policy* (Evanston, Illinois: Northwestern University Press, 1973), p. 26.

14. Ibid.

Chapter Seven

Epilogue

Almost 18 months after we ended our empirical investigation concerning the politics of evaluation at Opportunity Funding Corporation, we returned to re-examine some of our conclusions. We found that most of our original conclusions were reinforced and that the organization has continued to speak of itself as primarily interested in developing demonstration projects, while remaining primarily operationally oriented.

Jack Gloster, in discussing OFC objectives, noted that:

The broad objectives of OFC are: (1) to accumulate a body of experience on methods (primarily indirect financing techniques) of influencing private capital flow to poverty-area economic development activities, (2) to disseminate results and interpretations of lessons learned from its activities, and (3) to analyze the effectiveness of the OFC concept.

1. The accumulation of a body of experience requires that most of OFC's efforts will be directed at conducting demonstration programs and projects. Additional experience will be obtained through interaction with the private financial community, the low-income sector, and the government sector.

2. Results of OFC's activities will be communicated to all appropriate government agencies, financial community contacts and poverty community organizations as interim findings are made. Moreover, OFC will make recommendations for instituting its successful demonstrations in the government sector and the private sector wherever appropriate.

3. OFC will continue to study the effectiveness of its overall activities to determine whether or not the OFC concept as a whole should be institutionalized. It will also test the feasibility of self-sufficiency for OFC or segments of its operations. Finally, based on its experience OFC will modify its strategies and courses of

action when such changes would help achieve its objectives. Major amendments to the Business Plan affecting overall objectives, would be accomplished through consultation with OEO.[1]

Other than the Boone-Young case-study evaluation of the Surety Bonding Program and that of the Midwest Bank capital support project, there have been no outside evaluations of OFC programs. Of course, OFC is now required by OEO to perform its own semi-annual and annual "audit" of its activities. But, there has been no attempt since the Economic Innovation group withdrew from its evaluation function with OFC (in late 1972) to consider the design or implementation of a rigorous evaluation program. This is particularly significant because of the requirement that a valid evaluation develop a design prior to implementation of a project so that appropriate data-gathering facilities can be put in place and controls established prior to project operation. OFC has itself developed only relatively brief case studies of several of its projects.

OFC seems content to rely on several general measures in determining the relative effectiveness of its projects:

1. Failure rate;
2. Leverage rate of OFC funds—that is, the multiple that OFC assigns to funds that accrue to a project after the injection of an OFC guarantee, letter of credit, etc.
3. The degree to which others, in the private sector, will support OFC projects through their investments;
4. The degree to which federal agencies involved in minority economic development will adopt techniques developed by OFC.

OEO has likewise withdrawn from the fray and no longer insists on either project designs amenable to evaluation or a third-party evaluation of any kind. Of course OEO has passed through a period of extreme uncertainty (1971–73) about its own continuity as an institutional entity as well as experiencing a grave pressure on its budget. In fact, at the very time this Epilogue is being written, virtually all the parts of OEO have been spun off of the parent agency (viz. CAP agency to HEW, Legal Aid established as an independent quasi-public corporation, and the various manpower programs, that are still in existence, within the Labor Department). EDD also has gone through a long period of uncertainty as to its future and it was only decided in late 1974 that EDD would be moved to the Commerce Department as an independent department, not under OMBE.

Because of the institutional and funding pressures on EDD, it is not so surprising that it has not retained its early enthusiasm for a vigorous evaluation of OFC projects.

In terms of our ten specific propositions concerning the nature of the political impact on evaluation, design, operation, and result application, we find that there is little to add to our original conclusions. We feel these propositions still fairly represent the nature of the political impact on social program evaluation in the OFC context and hope that future researchers will indicate their relative generalizeability in other program settings.

In all fairness to the OFC staff and board of directors, it should be noted that a number of factors other than political considerations have militated against the development and implementation of a vigorous evaluation program. These factors include the following.

1. No money earmarked for evaluation has been provided to OFC by OEO or any other agency. Thus, all expenditures in this area by OFC would have to come from OFC operating funds. Resources have not even been provided to develop data gathering mechanisms or to place such mechanisms in place with OFC clients so that third party evaluation would be possible.

2. OEO, not OFC, is charged with the principal evaluation responsibility and they have done little, after their initial insistence on evaluatable, experimental designs, to contract for vigorous, objective, third-party evaluations.

3. The environment in which OFC projects must operate presents many variables that are difficult to control or isolate—that is, most of the OFC projects must operate, not in a laboratory, but in an open and dynamic market environment. In addition, OFC has little direct control over the parties to whom it provides guarantees and subsidies, since OFC funds generally form only a small portion of the capital base. Thus, vigorous evaluation design and implementation are inherently very difficult.

4. OFC provides only a small portion of its clients' capital—primarily indirect financing to its clients such as guarantees or letters of credit—and is thus only one party to a three or more party project, while for such experimental programs as Head Start or The New Jersey Wage Incentive the funding agency, HEW, was the primary source of direct program support.

5. Most of OFC clients are business organizations or others interested primarily in attaining some operational goal, without regard to economic development in the disadvantaged community. Further, these organizations have little understanding of evaluation and are run primarily by business people, not social scientists or academics.

In any case, OFC seems content to rely largely on the market acceptance of their programs taken as a whole to determine their relative effectiveness, rather than evaluations of their individual projects.

To the extent OFC can stimulate substantial investment by private sector organizations in poverty area economic development projects in which they are a party, they feel that such investment will be the primary measure of their success. Further, if agencies or organizations other than OEO are willing to invest directly in OFC, then they feel that this will indicate their credibility and effectiveness as a poverty area economic development catalyst. Finally, to the extent they can obtain concrete new legislative and/or administrative action by agencies directly involved in poverty area development, they will feel that they have fulfilled a major aim of influencing federal economic development policy to become more efficient.

A crucial frustration that remains to be answered is whether the present OFC self-evaluation will provide the kind of hard, objective data that will convince further private or public sector investment in OFC. The extent to which they will be able to obtain significant changes in legislation and/or administrative actions on the basis of little or no hard data is also an open question.

However, the authors remain convinced that many of the underlying OFC concepts about motivating greater private sector investment in poverty area economic development are viable and can work given the appropriate environment and sufficient resources to prove their value in a number of appropriately designed experimental programs.

NOTES

1. Jack Gloster, OFC Memorandum, "Draft of Business Plan," September 6, 1973, pp. 5–6.

Bibliography

BOOKS

Allen, Robert L. *Black Awakening in Capitalistic America: An Analytic History.*
Garden City, New York: Doubleday, 1970.
  The author has written about the possibilities for radical change
  in the socioeconomic status of blacks in American society. He
  discusses frankly the various palliatives currently being enacted and
  other proposals to solve the racial "problem."
Altshuler, Alan A. *Community Control.* New York: Pegasus Books, Inc., 1970.
  A sociological treatment of the black demand for political participation in large American cities is presented, with a focus on realistic
  options at this point in time.
Analysis of Little Business and the Little Business man of Philadelphia. Vols. I
  and II. Philadelphia: Drexel Institute of Technology, 1964.
  A report in Volume I on small black businessmen in Philadelphia
  and the accompanying appendix in Volume II combine to provide
  a very detailed analysis of black business in Philadelphia in the
  early 60's.
Andreason, Alan R. *Inner City Business: A Case Study of Buffalo, New York:*
  Praeger Publishers, September, 1971.
  This is a study of local business structure in the heavily black
  ghetto, with recommendations for planning inner-city business
  development. It examines Buffalo, where half of the retail service
  and other non-professional business studied are black owned.
  Appendix, tables, and figures.
Bailey, Ronald W. *Black Business Enterprise: Historical and Contemporary
  Perspectives.* New York: Basic Books, Inc., 1971.
  The author has provided a comprehensive sourcebook on black
  economic development, its history, its current status, and its future
  prospects. It contains twenty-six readings that present approaches to

137

the problem of black economic development, from complete separatism to full integration into the white economy, from attempts to build a viable black private enterprise sytem to various types of communal and state socialism and strategies of revolution.

Banfield, Edward C. *The Unheavenly City.* Boston: Little, Brown and Co., 1970.
A conservative political scientist's view of the nature of our urban dilemma and his proposed solutions for its amelioration are presented.

—— and James Q. Wilson. *City Politics.* New York: Vintage Books, 1963.
This classic book on how city government operates uses Daley's Chicago as one example of a type of political governance and to a lesser extent, other prototypes such as Dallas and Los Angeles.

Bardolph, Richard. *The Civil Rights Record: Black Americans and the Law 1849-1970.* New York: Crowell, 1970.
This is a story of a black man's struggle to achieve legal and Constitutional rights. A part of the story is written in the author's words, more of it in the words of the documents that made the silent revolution possible.

Bauer, Raymond A. *Social Indicators.* Cambridge: M.I.T. Press, 1966.
This book confronts the inadequate statistical guides on which government now relies for decision making. It enables us to assess where we stand and are going, with respect to our values and goals, and to evaluate specific programs and determine their impact.

Becker, Gary S. *The Economics of Discrimination.* Chicago: University of Chicago Press, 1971.
The author's work confronts discrimination in the market place because of race, religion, sex, color, social class, personality or other non-pecuniary considerations. Mr. Becker demonstrated that discrimination in the market place by any group reduces their own real incomes as well as those of the minority. He is also able to explain why the minority groups suffer much more from discrimination than do the majorities.

Bell, Carolyn S. *The Economics of the Ghetto.* New York: Pegasus Books, Inc., 1970.
This is an economist's view of the questions of income and poverty, housing, consumers and markets employments and education.

Bendix, Reinhard. *Embattled Reason: Essays on Social Knowledge.* New York: Oxford University Press, 1970.
A collection of sociological essays published over a twenty-year period is provided. The essays deal with changing historical experience.

Berry, Brian, Sandra Parsons, and Rutherford Platt. *The Impact of Urban Renewal on Small Business: The Hyde Park Kenwood Case.* Chicago: Center for Urban Studies, University of Chicago, 1968.
This case study of the Hyde Park/Kenwood area of Chicago and

the impact of federal renewal projects on small businessmen includes an analysis of the mortality experience of the displacees.

Birch, David L. *The Businessman and the City.* Boston: Graduate School of Business Administration, Harvard University, 1967.

This book contains the proceedings of a conference by leaders of the Harvard Business School Association to bring together businessmen, Harvard Business School faculty, and government officials, and to ask them to reach an understanding, first, as to what can be done to solve urban problems.

Blalock, Hubert M. *Causal Inferences in Non-experimental Research.* Chapel Hill: University of North Carolina Press, 1964.

This study attempts to pull together materials on causal inferences that are widely scattered in the philosophical, statistical, and social science literatures.

Blau, Peter M. *Dynamics of Bureaucracy; A Study of Interpersonal Relations in Two Government Agencies.* Chicago: University of Chicago Press, 1955.

The study contributes to the understanding of social interaction within the bureaucratic structure on the basis of an intensive investigation of small groups of officials in two government agencies.

Blaustein, Arthur I. and Geoffrey Faux. *The Star-Spangled Hustle.* New York: Doubleday, 1972.

This is an excellent, if somewhat biased, critique of the growth of the federal minority enterprise program written by two former OEO staff members.

Bolino, August C. *Manpower and the City.* Cambridge: Schenkman Publishing Co., 1969.

This book attempts to discuss the many manpower laws, their effectiveness, and their relationship to the broader society.

Bonjean, Charles M., Terry N. Clark, and Robert L. Lineberry (eds). *Community Politics: A Behavioral Approach.* New York: The Free Press, 1971.

This is a collection of readings on the structure of mass participation in community politics, elites and power structures, attitudes and values of community leaders, and the multiplicity of local governments.

Bower, Raymond A. and Scott M. Cunningham. *Studies in the Negro Market.* Cambridge: Marketing Science Institute, 1970.

This report has been compiled from a series of studies on the Negro market. The authors have explored distinctive aspects of Negro consumer behavior, response to advertising and the implications of these marketing phenomena. The black and white consumption patterns are examined to show differences in spending habits, shopping likes and dislikes, and their concern for buying well-known brands.

Bruyn, Severyn T. *Communities in Action, Pattern and Process.* New Haven: College and University Press, 1963.

What can be accomplished by aroused citizenry is exemplified by four variously successful cases of community "democracy" solving social problems—but the communities are mostly white and prosperous. The book has an "optimistic" flavor.

Bunge, Mario. *Causality*. Cambridge: Harvard University Press, 1959.

This book analyzes the meaning of the law of causation and makes a critical examination of the extreme claims that it opposes without restriction (causalism) and that it is an out-moded fetish (acusalism). The author has tried to do this by studying how the casual principle actually works in various departments of modern science.

Campbell, Donald T. and Julian C. Stanley. Experimental and Quasi-Experimental Designs for Research. Originally appeared in N.L. Gage (ed.), *Handbook of Research on Teaching*. Chicago: Rand McNally, 1963.

The study examines the validity of 16 experimental designs against 12 common threats to valid inference.

Caplovitz, David. *The Poor Pay More: Consumer Practices of Low Income Families*. New York: The Free Press, 1967.

This book examines consumers' practices among low-income families in New York City. It describes the major durables they own, how they went about getting them, and the difficulties they encountered along the way.

Caro, Francis G. *Readings in Evaluation Research*. New York: Russell Sage Foundation, 1971.

This book brings together material about evaluation research from a variety of sources. The readings include general statements about evaluation research and specific case materials. It is intended for students and professionals concerned with directed social change.

CDCs: New Hope for the Inner City. New York: The Twentieth Century Fund, 1971.

This is a report of the Twentieth Century Fund Task Force on Community Development Corporations that contains a condensed, easily understandable summary of findings and recommendations.

Chamberlain, Neil W. *Business and the Cities: A Look of Relevant Readings*. New York: Basic Books, 1970.

The 78 readings and documents included in this volume describe and evaluate business efforts in specific areas, ranging from manpower development and education and retraining to urban development and black capitalism. Some of the materials reproduced deal more with the background of the problems that business confronts than with the business role, and some are more descriptive than analytical.

—— and Donald E. Cullen. *The Labor Sector*. New York: McGraw-Hill, 1971.

The writers have drawn upon insights of various social sciences in an attempt to integrate the diverse studies of industrial relations.

Clark, Kenneth B. *Dark Ghetto: Dilemmas of Social Power*. New York: Harper and Row, 1965.

This book's emphasis on the pathologies of American ghettos

attempts to describe and interpret what happens to human beings who are confined to depressed areas and whose access to the normal channels of economic mobility and opportunity is blocked.

—— and Jeanette Hopkins. *A Relevant War Against Poverty.* New York: Harper Torchbooks, 1969.

The authors offer a prophecy of the future concerning the Johnsonian War on Poverty and other such programs based on their analysis of the planner's naivete in not understanding the nature of power and its use. Community participation is an ideal goal, but when thrust upon people unfamiliar with principles of participation democracy, it is unachievable.

Clark, Terry N. *Community Structure and Decision Making.* San Francisco: Chandler, 1968.

This book may become the standard sociological and descriptive treatise on the structural organization of communities. Not easy for the amateur sociologist to read.

Cleaver, Eldridge. *Soul on Ice.* New York: Bantam Books, 1968.

This eloquent book is one of the best statements of white racism's impact on the black man's personality and self-concept.

Cross, Theodore L. *Black Capitalism: Strategy for Business in the Ghetto.* New York: Atheneum, 1969.

This book is concerned with a different face of poverty—not the view that proclaims that almost everyone in the ghetto is poor—or rather the reverse face of poverty that states that almost nobody in the ghettos of America is rich, or even affluent. The author's thesis is that the ghetto economy operates at the threshold of anarchy. Therefore, it must be completely reshaped and stabilized.

Davis, James W., Jr., ed. *Politics, Programs and Budgets.* Englewood Cliffs, New Jersey: Prentice-Hall, 1969.

This book contains recent material on the growing use of economic analysis in budget making and on the connection between government programs and the government budget.

Denison, Edward F. *The Sources of Economic Growth in the United States and the Alternatives Before Us.* New York: Committee for Economic Development, 1962.

This study attempts to measure as exhaustively as possible, the sources of economic growth in the United States in the past fifty years and to appraise the implications of that experience for the future.

Doctors, Samuel I., ed. *Whatever Happened to Minority Enterprise.* Chicago: Dryden Press, 1974.

This book of original readings and case studies is based, largely, on the Chicago experience. It raises most of the difficult problems that need to be thoughtfully discussed for this rapidly growing, federally sponsored program.

—— and Anne S. Huff. *Minority Capitalism and the President's Council.* Boston: Ballinger, 1973.

This is a detailed analysis of the work of the President's Council
for Minority Business Enterprise and the effects of its recommendations on federal policy development.

Donovan, John. *The Politics of Poverty.* New York: Pegasus, 1967.

This study addresses itself to the questions that have to do with
the politics of poverty. It has been emphasized that the War on
Poverty is a product of an ongoing and complex political process,
one which begins long before the bill was introduced in the Congress.

Downs, Anthony. *Urban Problems and Prospects.* Chicago: Markham Publishing
Co., Inc., 1970.

A radical view of alternative futures for the American ghetto
with some insightful suggestions on how to achieve racial harmony.

Drucker, Peter. *The Age of Discontinuity.* New York: Harper and Row, 1969.

An "early-warning system," reporting discontinuities that while
still below the visible horizon, are already changing structure and
meaning of economy, polity, and society. It does not project trends.
It asks "What do we have to tackle today to make tomorrow?"

Durham, Laird. *Black Capitalism.* Washington, D.C.: Arthur D. Little, Inc.,
1970.

This incisive little book that attempts to explode some prevailing
"myths" concerning why black capitalism has failed. The author
then discusses his ideas for making black capitalism a viable strategy.

Elkins, Stanley. *Slavery.* Chicago: University of Chicago Press, 1968.

This brilliant dissertation on the effect of slavery on the historical
reluctance of black Americans to assert their rights compares the
psychology of slavery to concentration camp studies. This book
recently fell into disrepute because Daniel Moynihan drew upon
it to argue that "negro family pathology" was at the root of race
problems.

Ellis, William W. *White Ethics and Black Power.* Chicago: Aldine Publishing
Co., 1969.

This case study of Chicago's West Side Organization, a community
development organization in the Near West Side, shows how an
organization controlled by community residents is responsive to the
people's needs.

Elman, Richard M. *The Poorhouse State: The American Way of Public Assistance.*
New York: Dell, 1966.

This book provides a horrifying description of poor persons
caught in bureaucratic welfare machinery with its systematic
humiliation.

Epstein, Edwin M. and David R. Hampton eds. *Black Americans and White
Business.* Belmont, California: Dickenson Publishing Co., Inc., 1971.

This reader gives a social and economic perspective on the black
condition in America, plus the social and psychological implications
of contemporary racial attitudes; these two theoritical contributions
are then used to analyze the relationship of business institutions and
the black community.

Fairweather, George. *Methods for Experimental Social Innovation.* New York:
Wiley, 1967.

This book is offered as a beginning effort to bring the experimental methods of the social scientist to bear upon the pressing social problems of our time. It gives general experimental procedures from the inception of the ideas to publication and the planning of subsequent researches.

Fisher, Sir Ronald Aylmer. *The Design of Experiments.* New York: Hafner, 1966.

This book explains the principles of experimental designs in their simplest possible applications, which had been successful in many fields.

Foley, Eugene P. *The Achieving Ghetto.* Washington, D.C.: The National Press, Inc., 1968.

This book by a former SBA administrator is written about a subject that is of increasing importance: the economic development of the black ghetto.

Frazier, E. Franklin. *Black Bourgeoisie.* New York: Collier Books, 1968.

In an interesting look at the black middle class, Frazier contends that once a black "makes it" in the white world, he looks down on his former brothers in typical white middle-class disgust.

Gibson, D. Parke. *The $30 Billion Negro.* New York: Macmillan, 1969.

This book takes a look at only one dimension of Negro life in America—how Negroes act and react in the marketplace and what those who would sell goods and services or seek to shape thought and opinion should know about effectively motivating this consumer.

Ginzberg, Eli. *Business Leadership and the Negro Crisis.* New York: McGraw-Hill, 1968.

Eli Ginzberg and other noted contributors report on the current racial economic crisis. The report is divided into the following four sections: Perspectives—a background examination of the complexities of the problem; Political alternatives—society's role in fostering this dilemma and its responsibilities to correct the situation; Programs—speculative solutions to start ghetto businesses rolling; and Policy—the proposed action that business and government can take to assuage current economic bias.

Grebler, Leo, Joan W. Moore, and Ralph C. Guzman. *The Mexican-American People.* New York: The Free Press, 1970.

This most complete overview of the history of the Mexican-Americans includes a historical perspective of migration patterns, socioeconomic conditions, the individual in the social system, the role of churches (especially Catholic), and political interaction.

Greer, Scott A. *The Logic of Social Inquiry.* Chicago: Aldine Publishing Co., 1969.

The author formulates clearly what the social science looks to one practitioner. He shows both the relevance of the broadest philosophical questions to the research scientist and the relevance of his work to major questions concerning the human situation.

Haddad, William F. and G. Douglas Pugh, eds. *Black Economic Development.* Englewood Cliffs, New Jersey: Prentice-Hall, Inc., 1969.

This book provides a number of opinion papers on the problems

of black economic development by leading authorities and is one
of the early works in the field.

Hampden-Turner, Charles. *Radical Man.* Cambridge, Mass.: Schenkman Publishing Co., 1970.

The author attempts to model the human process of psycho-social
development and to lay the foundations of a humanistic psychology.

Hannerz, Ulf. *Soulside: Inquiries into Ghetto Culture and Community.* New
York: Columbia University Press, 1969.

Like William Whyte's classic study, Hannerz depicts urban ghetto
society in graphic detail from the vantage point of an observer living
in such a society. An excellent study of modern ghetto society and
culture that provides an important framework for any economic
solutions to the problems of urban poor.

Harris, Abraham L. *The Negro as Capitalist: A Study of Banking and Business
Among American Negroes.* Gloucester, Mass. Peter Smith, Inc.,
1968.

An examination of black banking and other businesses in the
United States, pinpointing the huge gap in deposits, capital, size,
and other variables between these enterprises and their counterpart
white firms.

Henderson, William L. and Larry C. Ledebur. *Economic Disparity.* New York:
The Free Press, 1970.

An overview of the problems of economic inequity with a comparison of moderate and militant solutions.

Hund, James M. *Black Entrepreneurship.* Belmont, California: Wadsworth
Publishing Co., 1970.

A good overview of the problem of black entrepreneurship and
possible future directions for minority economic development.

Jones, Edward H. *Blacks in Business.* New York: Grosset and Dunlap, 1971.

The author gives a brief history of the black businessman and a
guide to action. Not all black business concerns, he points out,
are small, or failures, but very few have enormous, continuing
success. Capital, credit, markets, competition, know-how, insurance,
and running a business concern, present special problems to blacks,
but with assistance and guidance, and with increased opportunity,
they can overcome these seemingly insuperable handicaps.

Kain, John F., ed. *Race and Poverty.* Englewood Cliffs, N.J.: Prentice-Hall, Inc.,
1969.

This book contains readings on the economic condition of the
Negro, the labor market and discrimination, the housing market,
attitudes toward race and police alternatives for solving the problem·

Kerner Commission Report. Washington, D.C.: U.S. Government Printing
Office, June 1967.

This shocking report presents the causes of urban unrest with
some excellent, difinitive strategies for correcting the underlying
problems.

Kotler, Milton. *Neighborhood Government.* New York: Bobbs-Merrill, 1969.

This author argues for community control of all institutions that directly affect the lives of the residents; decision making on the economic structure of the community (localism) should emanate from the community.

Lazarsfeld, Paul F. and Morris Rosenberg, eds. *The Language of Social Research: A Reader in the Methodology of Social Research.* Glencoe, Ill.: The Free Press, 1955.

This comprehensive readings book on methodology of social research contains detailed sections on concepts, multivariate analysis, analysis of change through time, research on human groups, analysis of action, and philosophy of the social sciences.

Leeds, Ruth I. and Thomasina J. Smith, (eds.) *Using Social Science Knowledge in Business & Industry.* Homewood, Ill.: Richard D. Irwin, 1963.

The authors integrate the papers and discussion of the seminar held by the Foundation for Research on Human Behavior. The book focuses on the use of social science knowledge in business and industry that would strengthen the bridge between producers and the prospective users of social science knowledge.

Levitan, Sar. A. *Federal Aid to Depressed Areas.* Baltimore: Johns Hopkins Press, 1964.

This study examines the various components of the area redevelopment program, describing its operation, mainly from a Washington vantage point, and evaluates the activities for the Area Development Administration during the first two years.

———, Cohen, Wilbur J., and Robert J. Hampman, eds. *Towards Freedom from Want.* Madison, Wisconsin: Industrial Relations Research Assoc., 1968.

The authors emphasize the point that society's efforts to aid the poor have not been commensurate with its resources or the needs of the poor. Doubts are also raised as to whether the increased emphasis on helping the poor, the so-called "War on Poverty," has been effective.

———, Mangum, G.L., and Robert Taggart, III. *Economic Opportunity in the Ghetto: The Partnership of Government and Business.* Baltimore: Johns Hopkins Press, 1970.

This study is an analysis of joint government–business efforts. It describes their successes and failures to date and projects their potential impact.

——— and Irving H. Siegel. *Dimensions of Manpower Policy: Programs and Research.* Baltimore: The Johns Hopkins Press, 1966.

This volume commemorates completion of the first two decades of service of Upjohn Institute for Employment Research. It conveys the range and diversity of the Institute's research activity.

Mack, Raymond W. *Planning on Uncertainty: Decision Making in Business and Government Administration.* New York: John Wiley and Sons, 1971.

Addressing itself to the problems of business and government

policy making, the study explores the essential implications of the
fact that uncertainty is ubiquitous.

Marris, Peter and Martin Rein. *Dilemmas of Social Reform.* New York: Atherton
Press, 1967.

This is a scholarly, dispassionate and thorough report of the
frustrations and entanglements into which specific federal reform
projects have fallen.

Mason, Anthony. *Black Capitalism: Rhetoric and Reality.* New York: Equity
Research Associates, October 1969.

The picture that emerges from the report is one of men and organizations moving at cross-purposes; of giant corporations making
gestures that are often ill-conceived; of political maneuvering that
concels out what efficiency might have been inherent in a given
plan.

McLuhan, Marshall H. and Quentin Fiore. *The Medium is the Massage.* New
York: Bantam Books, 1967.

It is impossible to understand social and cultural changes that
are taking place currently without a knowledge of the workings of
media. This book is a look-around to see what's happening. It is
a kaleidoscope of interfaced situations.

Merton, Robert K. *Social Theory and Social Structure,* rev. ed. Glencoe, Ill.:
The Free Press, 1957.

The papers which make up the book have been assembled with
an eye to the gradual unfolding and developing of two sociological
concerns: first, with the interplay of social theory and social research,
and second, with progressively codifying both substantive theory
and the procedures of sociological analysis, most to qualitative
analysis.

Minar, David W. and Scott Greer, eds. *The Concept of Community.* Chicago:
Aldine Publishing Co., 1969.

This is a reader on the concept of community, the different kinds
of communities, the relationship of politics and community, community and social change, and the personal consequences of change.

Moynihan, Daniel P. *Maximum Feasible Misunderstanding.* New York: The
Free Press, 1969.

This is a discussion of the dynamics related to community action
and participation in the War on Poverty. This conservative theorist
argues that the poor may never be ready to assume power in
advanced society.

Myrdal, Gunnar. *An American Dilemma.* New York: Harper & Row, 1944,
1962.

The monumental study of black/white relations in the United
States prepared on the eve of the many changes that were about to
be wrought on this relationship in the aftermath of World War II,
the Korean War and the riots of the sixties. This is must reading
for anyone who wants to gain historical perspective on the cultural
problems created by our dual society.

——. *Challenge to Affluence.* New York: Pantheon Books, 1963.

  The author discusses the stagnating American economy and shows what are the implications, domestic and international, of this stagnation. He states that a growing economy could not coexist with the kind of poverty that has been allowed. He asks what will happen to the precarious gains made by the Negroes in a society where piecemeal reform is no longer able to prevent the growth of an "under class."

Nathan, Robert R. *Jobs and Civil Rights.* Washington, D.C.: U.S. Commission on Civil Rights, April 1969.

  This book provides a comprehensive look at anti-discrimination legislation and its impact on opening up job opportunities for minorities. Nathan gives very low grades to present federal enforcement policies in the fair employment area.

Ofairi, Earl. *The Myth of Black Capitalism.* New York: Monthly Review Press, 1970.

  This book provides a serious and enlightening background to current discussions about "Black Capitalism." The author has no sympathy for current efforts to promote black capitalism; he considers this a program of the black elite who, while very weak, would like to become stronger through exploitation of the black ghetto.

Ordiorne, George S. *Green Power: The Corporation and the Urban Crisis.* New York: Pitman Publishing Corporation, 1969.

  The author examines the problems of the urban crisis from all angles: the present methods of dealing with them, and the alternatives, such as massive federal government intervention, riot control, Black Power, and others. He offers a solution that is both simple and persuasive. He cogently argues that it is up to private business, to those who would preserve the system because they own or run it, to give those who do not—the poor—a stake in our society.

Pearl, Arthur and Frank Reissman. *New Careers for the Poor.* New York: The Free Press, 1965.

  This is an excellent treatment of potential strategies for hiring and training the "unemployable" in higher-growth areas to promote minority economic development.

Piven, Francis F. and Richard A. Cloward. *Regulating the Poor: The Functions of Public Welfare.* New York: Pantheon Books, 1972.

  This is an excellent description and analysis of the development of public welfare during two periods of "explosive" growth—the depression and the 1960s.

Pinkney, Alphonso. *Black Americans.* Englewood Cliffs, N.J.: Prentice-Hall, 1969.

  This study presents a reasonably complete picture of the status of black people in the United States at the present time. It begins with their first arrival in 1619 and continues up to the present crisis in race relations. Included is a section on black people in business.

Polsky, N.W. *Community Power and Political Theory.* New Haven, Conn.:
  Yale University Press, 1963.
    This is a classic academic treatise on community decision making—
    it supports the plurastic view against centralized planning.
Price, Don K. *The Scientific State.* Cambridge, Mass.: Harvard University Press,
  1965.
    This book contains the Page–Barbour Lectures delivered at
    Charlottesville in March 1963. This book adds perspective to the
    author's experience in the Ford Foundation where it was clear that
    political freedom does not depend altogether on technical assistance
    or skills drawn from sciences. It also adds perspective of collabora-
    tion with scholars from a number of academic disciplines.
Rainwater, L., and William L. Yancy. *The Moynihan Report and the Politics of
  Controversy.* Cambridge, Mass.: the M.I.T. Press, 1967.
    This is an excellent case study of how "custodial liberalism"
    operates and how angry it makes black leaders. In this case, Moyni-
    han used "mental health" perspectives to argue that the Negro
    family was often pathological. True? Possibly, but the road to hell
    is paved with research findings; do you emancipate people with
    perspectives that label them inferior? The book consists of the
    report, rebuttals, and communts.
Ross, Arthur M. and Herbert Hill (eds.). *Employment, Race and Poverty.*
  New York: Harcourt, Brace and World, 1967.
    This book deals with the economic disabilities of Negro workers
    and the stakes and possibilities involved in economic integration.
    Included are articles written by different authors under these
    categories: The Negro Position in the Labor Market; The Social
    Effects of Negro Unemployment; The Means and Expressions of
    Protest Employers, Unions, and the Negro; Education and Training
    of the Negro; and Discrimination and the Law.
Ryan, William. *Blaming the Victim.* New York: Vintage Books, 1971.
    The purpose of this book is to persuade the reader that many of
    his friends and neighbors—and perhaps even he himself—have been
    tricked into believing many lies about the social and economic
    injustice that infects all parts of American life and, second, to
    provide him with a viewpoint and a method of analysis that can
    armour him against future tricks and lies.
Samora, Julian (ed.). *La Raza: Forgotten Americans.* South Bend, Indiana:
  Notre Dame Press, 1966.
    This collection of readings is on the Mexican–American experience
    in the United States, identifying specific ethnic characteristics
    that have molded what little economic development that they
    have experienced.
Secord, Paul F. and Carl W. Beckman. *Social Psychology.* New York: McGraw-
  Hill, 1964.
    The field of social psychology has been usefully covered by

attempting to weave together the contributions of the fields of psychology and sociology.

Seidman, Harold. *Politics, Position and Power: The Dynamics of Federal Organization.* Washington, D.C.: Oxford University Press, 1970.

This book records the author's observations of the various phenomena that determine and influence federal organization structure and administrative arrangements. It depicts the federal scene as observed for almost a quarter of a century through the Bureau of Budget.

Sethi, S. Prahash. *Business Corporations and the Black Man.* Cranton, Penn.: Chandler Publishing Co., 1970.

This book is an analysis of social conflict: The Kodak–Fight controversy. It developed out of the author's studies on the role of business corporations in a changing social system. Business corporations today find themselves confronted by new groups, especially those representing minorities, who question the social value of the economic services and corporations perform, whose demands defy long-accepted criteria of economic efficiency, and whose strategies and tactics seem to violate all the rules of the game.

Silberman, Charles E. *Crisis in Black and White.* New York: Vintage, 1964.

This is probably the best popular account of race relationships written by a white man. One of the first books to advocate "Poor Power" and praise the Woodlawn Organization for its fight against the expansion of the University of Chicago.

Simon, Herbert A. *Administrative Behavior.* New York: Macmillan, 1957.

This book is an important contribution to social science of formal organization and administration. The object is to construct a set of tools—a set of concepts and a vocabulary—suitable for describing an organization and the way an administrative organization works.

Slater, Philip E. *The Pursuit of Loneliness.* Boston: Beacon Press, 1970.

The book provides some understanding of the social and psychological forces that are pulling the American society apart. The author talks about what people do to themselves and to each other.

Sovern, Michael I. *Legal Restraints on Racial Discrimination in Employment.* New York: Twentieth Century Fund, 1966.

This book contains a thorough look at the development of state and federal anti-discrimination (in employment) statutes, and is written in a style that the layman can understand.

Spear, Allan H. *Black Chicago.* Chicago: University of Chicago Press, 1967.

An in-depth statistical and psychological examination is given to Chicago's black population and its characteristics.

Sturdivant, Frederick D., ed. *The Ghetto Marketplace.* New York: The Free Press, 1969.

This book contains a collection of articles about the "incongruity created by the ghetto environment for the consumer." It is a marketplace in which the unwary poor are often victims of unethical or illegal merchandising ". . . [and in which] retailers who do try to serve their customers are faced with such problems as high operating costs and, often, community resentment."

Suchman, Edward A. *Evaluative Research.* New York: Russell Sage Foundation, 1968.

Much of the book is concerned with difficult evaluative problems. It provides significant increment of technical knowledge for evaluative research person. The author has achieved a striking balance between rigorous design and method and the situational realities in which one must function.

Tabb, William T. *The Political Economy of the Black Ghetto.* New York: W.W. Norton, 1970.

The purpose of this book is to describe the economic factors which help explain the origins of the black ghetto and the mechanisms through which exploitations and deprivation are perpetuated; and to explore strategies for ending them.

Webb, Eugene J. et al. *Unobtrusive Measures: Non-Reactive Research in the Social Sciences.* Chicago: Rand-McNally, 1966.

Physical evidence, secondary data, and simple observation are suggested as alternatives and supplements to interviews and questionnaires in social science research. These measures minimize the need for cooperation from the subject and lessen the possibility that the measurement process with change either the subject or the phenomenon.

Weber, Max. *Economy and Society: An Outline of Interpretive Sociology.* New York: Bedminster Press, 1968. Writings edited by Guenther Roth and Claus Wittich.

This is the first strictly empirical comparison of social structure and normative order in world-historical depth.

——. *Essays in Sociology.* New York: Oxford University Press, 1946.

This is an excellent translation of Max Weber's works and speeches by H.H. Garth and C.W. Mills. It contains sections on Weber's life and work, science and politics, power, religion, and social structures.

Weiss, Carol H. *Evaluating Action Programs: Readings in Social Action and Education.* Boston: Allyn and Bacon, 1972.

The book helps the reader conceptualize and understand the purposes of evaluation and the methods by which it obtains information and generates conclusions.

Wholey, Joseph S. et al. *Federal Evaluation Policy: Analyzing the Effects of Public Programs.* Washington, D.C.: Urban Institute, 1970.

This book reports the Urban Institute's study of federal evaluation policies and concentrates on the organizational framework, the methodologies and the amount of federal resources used at the time the review began in late 1968.

Wildavsky, Aaron B. *The Politics of the Budgetary Process.* Boston: Little, Brown and Co., 1964.

The author describes the kinds of calculation made in budgeting and the types of strategies the participants use to accomplish their purposes. He appraises budgetary process and suggest alternatives based on descriptive material.

ARTICLES

Aronson, Sidney H. and Clarence C. Sherwood. "Researcher Versus Practitioner: Problems in Social Action Research," in C.H. Weiss (ed.), *Evaluating Action Programs.* Boston: Allyn and Bacon, Inc., 1972., pp. 283–93.
>   This article reviews the efforts of the research branch of an organization—Opportunities for Youth (OFY)—to evaluate a group of demonstration programs.

Bahn, Anita K. "Research Tools for Planning and Evaluation," in Richard H. Williams and Lucy D. Ozarin (eds.), *Community Mental Health.* San Francisco: Jossen-Bass, Inc., 1968, pp. 292–304.
>   The author reviews some uses and limitations of psychiatric case registers and briefly refers to the potential contributions from the population survey.

Belletire, Michael and Samuel Doctors. "Education and Training: The Missing Ingredient in Minority Capitalism," *Journal of Small Business Management,* (Fall 1973), pp. 11–16.
>   The importance of management education and training to the success of minority enterprises is discussed.

Bigman, Stanley K. "Evaluating the Effectiveness of Religious Programs," *Review of Religious Research,* Vol. 2, No. 1, 1960, pp. 97–121.
>   This paper is concerned with evaluation research: its major phases, some of the special problems arising in program evaluation, and some of the types of studies that might be made of ongoing activities conducted by religious bodies.

"Black Capitalism: Problems and Prospects," a special issue, *Saturday Review,* (August 23, 1969), pp. 15–29.
>   These articles focus on the need to intensify ghetto economic development while maintaining momentum toward integration; describe how ghetto capitalism has served succeeding waves of ethnic groups but so far has failed black Americans; evaluate possible government-business programs of "compensatory capitalism"; and include "The New Black Businessman."

Blau, Peter. "The Empirical Study of Bureaucratic Structure and Function," in David R. Hampton et al. (eds.), *Organizational Behavior and the Practice of Management.* Glenview, Ill.: Scott Foresman, 1968, pp. 72–81.
>   Discusses the method of studying informal processes of organizational development on the basis of an examination of the daily operations and the interpersonal relations of government officials.

Campbell, Donald T. "Comments on the Comments of Shaver and Staines,"
    Urban Affairs Quarterly, Vol. 7, No. 2 (December 1971), pp. 187–
    192.
    The author suggests to the social scientists that they participate
    as methodologists in evaluating the innovations that the political
    process produces, thereby foregoing their theoretical interests
    for practical purposes.
——. "Reforms as Experiments," *Urban Affairs Quarterly,* Vol., No. 2 (Decem-
    ber 1971), pp. 133–71.
    The theme of this article is that most amelioration programs end
    up with no interpretable evaluation. Many of the difficulties lie
    in the intransigencies of the research setting and in the presence of
    recurrent seductive pitfalls of interpretation.
——. "Considering the Case Against Experimental Evaluations of Social Innova-
    tions," *Administrative Science Quarterly,* Vol. 15, No. 1, 1970,
    pp. 110–3.
    It is a comment on the article "The Evaluation of Broad-Aim
    Programs: Experimental Design, its Difficulties, and An Alternative"
    by Weiss and Rein published in this issue. There are often weak-
    nesses in would-be experimental program evaluations, and Weiss and
    Rein usefully call attention to some of those weaknesses.
Campbell, Donald C. and A. Erlebacher. "How Regression Artifacts in Quasi-
    Experimental Evaluation Can Mistakenly Make Compensatory
    Education Look Harmful," in D. Hellmuth (ed.). *Compensatory
    Education: A National Debate.* New York: Brunner-Mazel, 1970.
Caporaso, James A. "Quasi-Experimental Approaches to Social Science: Per-
    spectives and Problems," in J.A. Caporaso and L.L. Roos, Jr. (eds.),
    *Quasi-Experimental Approaches: Testing Theory and Evaluating
    Policy.* Evanston, Ill.: Northwestern University Press, 1973, pp. 3–
    38.
    The objections and rationale for a quasi-experimental approach
    to social research are discussed.
Caro, Francis G. "Approaches to Evaluative Research—A Review," *Human
    Organization,* Vol. 28, No. 2 (Summer 1969), pp. 87–99.
    This represents an attempt to identify the major themes in
    recent social science literature with direct implications for evaluation
    research. The author focuses on situations in which action programs
    are conducted by formal organizations and evaluative researchers
    are directly linked to program administrators.
Carstairs, G.M. "Problems of Evaluative Research" in J. Williams and C. Orjarin
    (eds.). *Community Mental Health.* (San Francisco, Jossey-Boss),
    1968.
    The author presents an overview of the problems in evaluative
    research. He discusses different methods of evaluation and their
    relative merits.
Carter, Reginald K. "Clint's Resistance to Negative Findings and the Latent

Conservative Function of Evaluation Studies," *The American Sociologist,* Vol. 6, No. 2 (1971), pp. 118–24.

The author reports through case histories how resistance at the top management level to the findings of social science research evaluations were overcome.

Cohen, David K. "Politics and Research: Evaluation of Social Action Programs in Education," in C.H. Weiss (ed.), *Evaluating Action Programs.* Boston: Allyn and Bacon, 1972, pp. 137–65.

This article delineates the political character of the major new evaluation programs, reviews some evaluations of new programs, and suggests some elements of a strategy that might improve evaluation of social action programs.

Cook, T.J. and F.P., Scioli, Jr. "A Research Strategy for Analyzing the Impacts of Public Policy," *Administrative Science Quarterly,* Vol. 17, No. 3, (1972), pp. 328–39.

The authors present a research strategy for measuring policy impacts based upon the principles of experimental design methodology. The overall approach is discussed in terms of its general utility for policy impact analysis.

Davis, Keith E. and Edward E. Jones. "Changes in Interpersonal Perception as a Means of Reducing Cognitive Dissonance," *Journal of Abnormal and Social Psychology,* Vol. 61, No. 3, (1960), pp. 402–10.

The study is designed to demonstrate that dissonance produced by inconsistencies between one's evaluation of another and one's behavior toward him would be reduced, under certain conditions only, by changing one's evaluation to conform to the behavior.

Deniston, O.L., I.M. Rosenstock, and V.A. Getting. "Evaluation of Program Effectiveness," *Public Health Reports,* Vol. 83, No. 4 (April 1968), pp. 323–35.

The authors explain the systematic, comprehensive approach that is needed to evaluate the effectiveness of programs in public health.

Doctors, Samuel I. and Anthony Akel M. "Federal R & D Expenditures and Industrial Productivity," *Business Perspectives* (Summer 1973), pp. 17–27.

The benefits of federal R/D expenditures have been concentrated within a few industries and geographical areas. The authors argue that greater attention whould be given to technology transfer programs.

—— and Gordon Andrew. "Evaluation Strategy for a Social Action Program: The Opportunity Funding Corporation," *Urban and Social Change Review* (Fall 1972), pp. 22–28.

—— and Sharon Lockwood. "Opportunity Funding Corporation: An Analysis," *Law and Contemporary Problems* XXXVI, No. 2 (Spring 1971), pp. 227–237.

This article analyzes the initiation of the Opportunity Funding Corporation.

—— and Sharon Lockwood. "New Directions for Minority Enterprise" *Law and Contemporary Problems* XXXVI, No. 2, (Winter 1971), pp. 51–67.

    This article details the need for a more strategic, higher growth opportunity approach to minority enterprise development.

Evans, John W. "Head Start: Comments on the Criticisms," in Francis G. Caro (ed.), *Readings in Evaluation Research.* New York: Russell Sage Foundation, 1971, pp. 401–7.

    The author sets forth the reasons why the criticisms of the Westinghouse study of Head Start was of very limited validity in the context of evaluating ongoing social action programs.

——, "Evaluating Social Action Programs," *Social Science Qtr.,* Vol. 50 (Dec. 1969), pp. 568–581.

    The author cites several reasons for the lack of objective and empirical evaluations of social action programs.

—— and Walter Williams. "The Politics of Evaluation: The Case of Head Start," *The Annals of the American Academy of Political and Social Science,* Vol. 385, No. 5 (September 1969), pp. 118–32.

    This paper traces both the events that led up to the controversy over the Westinghouse Research Corporation–Ohio University evaluation of Head Start and the controversy itself in order to look at the implications for future evaluation policy.

Faux, Geoffrey. "Politics and Bureaucracy in Community Controlled Economic Development," *Law and Contemporary Problems,* Vol. 36, No. 2 (Spring 1971), pp. 277–96.

    The article discusses the essential ingredients to effective economic development in poverty areas.

Festinger, Leon, "A Theory of Social Comparison Processes," *Human Relations,* Vol. 7, No. 2 (1954), pp. 117–40.

    The author further develops previously published theory concerning opinion influence processes in social groups.

——, "Informal Social Communication," *Psychological Review,* Vol. 57, No. 4 (October 1950), pp. 271–82.

    This article provides a statement of the theoretical formulations developed in the process of conducting a program of empirical and experimental research in informal social communication.

—— and J.M. Carlsmith, "Cognitive Consequences of Forced Compliance," *Journal of Abnormal and Social Psychology,* Vol. 58, No. 2 (1959), pp. 203–10.

    Two derivations from the theory of cognitive dissonance were tested. The results strongly corroborated the theory.

Freeman, A. Myrick, III. "Project Design and Evaluation with Multiple Objectives," in R.M. Haveman and J. Margolis, *Public Expenditure and Policy Analysis.* Chicago: Markham Publishing Co., 1970, pp. 347–63.

The paper explores the shape of the dilemma of different views of objectives and allocating limited government budgets among competing programs and examines the progress in finding possible solutions at the practical level.

Friesema, H. Paul, "Urban Studies and Action Research," *Urban Affairs Quarterly,* Vol. 7, No. 1 (September 1971), pp. 3–11.

The author suggests that while the self-consciously urban-oriented academic community has yet to change the world very much, this special evolving community has surely shifted its own goals and community.

Gans, Herbert, "The Uses of Poverty: The Poor Pay All," *Social Policy,* Vol. 2, No. 2 (July/August 1971), pp. 20–4.

This article describes important functions that poverty and the poor satisfy in the American society. It supports functionalist thesis that poverty survives in part because it is useful to society.

Gardner, Reginald K., "Clients Resistance to Negative Findings and the Latent Conservative Function of Evaluation Studies," *The American Sociologist,* Vol. (May 1971), pp. 118–124.

When the findings of an evaluation conflict with the values, beliefs, or reward system of the client, resistance is likely. Several suggestions are offered for avoiding this situation before the evaluation is begun.

Gordon, Andrew C., "University-Community Relations: Problems and Prospects," in *Cities in Change: Studies on the Urban Condition,* John Walton and Donald E. Carns, eds. Boston: Allyn & Bacon, 1973), pp. 549–572.

A discussion with examples of the problems and opportunities for academic involvement in social program evaluation.

Hyman, Herbert H. and Charles R. Wright. "Evaluating Social Action Programs," in Francis G. Caro (ed.), *Readings in Evaluation Research.* New York: Russell Sage Foundation, 1971, pp. 185–220.

Concern is with the methodology of evaluation research and the general contribution that a social-science orientation can make to the evaluation of social action programs.

Johnson, L. and W. Smith. "Black Managers," *Black Economic Development.* Englewood Cliffs, N.J.: Prentice Hall, 1969, pp. 112–25.

The article briefly reviews the limited history of the black businessman and makes some suggestions that will lead to black managers of successful businesses.

Jones, E.E. and K.E. Davis. "From Acts to Disposition," in Leonard Berkowitz (ed.), *Advances in Experimental Social Psychology.* New York: Academic Press, 1965, pp. 219–266.

The authors introduce the notion of explaining an action by assigning an intention and to set the stage for the theory of inference that follows.

Longood, Robert and Arnold Simmel. "Organizational Resistance to Innovation
    Suggested by Research," in C.H. Weiss (ed.), *Evaluating Action
    Programs.* Boston: Allyn and Bacon, 1972, pp. 311–17.
        The paper discusses the tendencies to resist innovation that
    are rooted in the nature of organizations and society.
Mangum, Garth L. "Evaluating Manpower Programs," in *Employment and
    Training Legislation–1968,* prepared by the Subcommittee on
    Employment, Manpower and Poverty of the Committee on Labor
    and Public Welfare. Washington, D.C.: U.S. Senate, 1968.
        The article discusses programs and practices that can be analyzed
    in aggregate and from which policy emphases can be extracted.
McKersie, Robert B. "Vitalize Black Enterprise," *Harvard Business Review*
    (September–October 1968), pp. 88–99.
        The author shows how efforts by corporations to hire and train
    unemployed Negro so far have only scratched the surface of the
    problem, and he discusses the essential elements necessary to
    vitalize black enterprise in terms of a promising corporation-spon-
    sored organization in one of the cities.
Merton, Robert K. "The Role of Applied Social Science in the Formulation
    of Policy," *Philosophy of Science,* Vol. 16 (July 1949), pp. 161–81.
        Conditions limiting and making the achievements of social science,
    and the theoretic and methodological by-products of research in
    applied social science are discussed.
——. "The Unanticipated Consequences of Purposive Social Action," *The
    American Sociological Review,* Vol. 1 (December 1936), pp. 894–
    904.
        This paper largely deals with the problems of unanticipated
    consequences of isolated purposive acts rather than with their
    integration into a coherent system of action.
—— and E.C. Devereux. "Practical Problems and the Use of Social Science,"
    Transaction, Vol. 1, No. 5 (July 1964), pp. 18–21.
        The article explores a few conditions that affected the demand for
    social research during the early stages of its use in the American
    Telephone and Telegraph Company.
—— and Daniel Lerner. "Social Scientists and Research Policy," in Daniel
    Lerner and Harold D. Lasswell (eds.), *The Policy Sciences.* Stanford:
    Stanford University Press, 1951, pp. 282–307.
        The ways in which men of knowledge influence the society in
    which it operates are discussed.
Miller, S.M. "The Study of Man: Evaluating Action Programs," *Transaction,*
    Vol. 2, No. 3 (March–April 1965), pp. 38–39.
        The author discusses the needs and problems of evaluation
    research.
Mitchell, Bert. "The Black Minority in the C.P.A. Profession," *The Journal of
    Accountancy* LLXXVIII, No. 10 (October 1969), pp. 41–48.
        The author, a member of the ALCPA committee on recruitment
    for disadvantaged groups, shows that the number of black CPAs is

disproportionately small and urges the accounting profession to make available real opportunities for the entry of minority groups into accounting.

Moskowitz, Milton R. "Opportunity Funding Corporation: Reversing the Poverty Cycle," *The Bankers Magazine,* Vol. 154, No. 4 (Autumn 1971), pp. 43–48.

This article discusses what the opportunity funding corporation can do to build the power of the poor to bid for capital resources and for technical assistance.

Roberts, Edward B. "Entrepreneurship and Technology," in William Gruber and Donald Marquis (eds.), *Factors in Technology Transfer.* Cambridge, Mass.: The M.I.T. Press, 1969, pp. 219–37.

Increasingly the recognized distinction between invention and innovation has been attributed to the personal role of the innovator, the individual who has acted to champion the translation of science and technology from laboratory into use. This paper is aimed at furthering the understanding of this personally based technical innovation process.

Roos, Noralou P. "Evaluation, Quasi-Experimentation and Public Policy," in J.A. Caporaso and L.L. Roos, Jr. (eds.), *Quasi-Experiments: Testing Theory and Evaluating Policy.* Evanston, Ill.: Northwestern University Press, 1973, pp. 281–304.

This is an attempt to develop a general framework for examining threats to the validity and utility of evaluation research.

Samuels, Howard J. "Compensatory Capitalism," in William F. Haddad and G. Douglas Pugh (eds.), *Black Economic Development.* Englewood Cliffs, N.J.: Prentice-Hall, 1969, pp. 60–73.

The author emphasizes the notion that American private enterprise must be transplanted and developed in the ghetto to provide it with the essential requirements for achieving its proportional share in the American business system.

Shaver, Phillip and Graham Staines. "Problems Facing Campbell's 'Experimenting Society,' " *Urban Affairs Quarterly,* Vol. 7, No. 2 (December 1971), pp. 173–86.

This paper represents comments made by the authors at a colloquium centered around a talk by Donald T. Campbell entitled "Experiments as Reforms."

"Social Programs, Social Sciences and Evaluation Research," *National Academy of Science News Report,* Vol. XXI, No. 9 (November 1971), pp. 1, 4–5.

This article reports on the questions of evaluation of federal programs that have remained thorny ones, particularly on the area of social programs and social experiments.

Solow, Robert M. "Technical Change and the Aggregate Productions Function," *Review of Economics and Statistics,* XXXIX, No. 3 (August 1957), pp. 312–20.

This paper has suggested a simple way of segregating shifts of the

aggregate production function from movements along it. The
methods rest on the assumption that factors are paid their marginal
products, but it could be extended to monopolistic factor markets.

Suchman, Edward A. "Principles and Practice of Evaluative Research," in
John T. Doby (ed.), *An Introduction to Social Research.* New York:
Appleton-Century-Crofts, 1967, pp. 327–51.

The author explains the principles and techniques of evaluative
research as one possible avenue for the development of a more
productive experimental sociology, and for the more traditional
use of evaluation to determine the success or failure of applied
programs of social action.

"The Nation's 100 Top Black Businesses," *Black Enterprise* III,
No. 11, (June 1973), pp. 29–35.

The report discusses how the black-owned and controlled firms
have fared since the period when black capitalism became a battle
cry for black participation in the economic mainstream of America.

Ward, David A. and Gene G. Kassebaum. "On Biting the Hand that Feeds: Some
Implications of Sociological Evaluations of Correctional Effective-
ness," in C.H. Weiss (ed.), *Evaluating Action Programs.* Boston:
Allyn and Bacon, 1972, pp. 300–10.

The authors raise some points for discussion regarding not the
whole process involved in assessing correctional effectiveness, but
mainly the things that happen after the study is reported. They
describe briefly the design and principal findings of investigation.

Webb, Eugene J. "Unconventionality, Triangulation, and Inference," in Norman
K. Denzin (ed.), *Sociological Methods.* Chicago: Aldine Publishing
Co., 1970, pp. 449–57.

This article stresses the utility of different data-gathering techniques
applied concurrently to the same problem and laying of these
techniques against multiple samples which are natural outcroppings
of a phenomenon.

Weiss, Carol H. "Where Politics and Evaluation Research Meet," *Evaluation*
I, No. 3 (1973), pp. 37–45.

Uniquely rational approaches that only appear to be irrational
are the subject of this investigation into the political context of
evaluation research.

——. "Utilization of Evaluation: Toward Comparative Study," in C.H. Weiss
(ed.), *Evaluating Action Programs.* Boston: Allyn and Bacon, 1972,
pp. 318–26.

The author addresses the problem of frequent failure of decision
makers to use the conclusions of evaluation research in setting
future directions for action programs.

——. "The Politicization of Evaluation Research," *Journal of Social Issues,*
Vol. 26, No. 4 (Autumn 1970), pp. 57–68.

This article discusses the political overtones of evaluation research
and its implications and reports the difficulties of evaluation research.

It begins with those difficulties that have to do with the method itself and then turns to those that have to do with the relationship between the research group and administrative group which the method imposes.

Weise, Robert S. and Martin Rein. "The Evaluation of Broad-Aim Programs: Difficulties in Experimental Design and an Alternative," in Carol Weiss (ed.) *Evaluating Action Progress.* (Boston, Allyn and Bacon) 1972.

The authors are primarily concerned with policy decisions. They see the need for information less in terms of data on comparative outcomes of programs and more in terms of understanding the forces that shape community programs.

Wildavsky, Aaron B. "The Political Economy of Efficiency: Cost–Benefit Analysis, Systems Analysis and Program Budgeting," in James W. Davis (ed.), *Politics, Programs, and Budgets.* Englewood Cliffs, N.J.: Prentice-Hall, 1969, pp. 230–52.

This paper takes the newest and recently most popular modes of achieving efficiency—cost benefit analysis, systems analysis, and program budgeting—and shows how much more is involved than mere economizing.

Williams, Walter. "Developing an Evaluation Strategy for a Social Action Agency," *Journal of Human Resources,* Vol. IV, No. 4 (Fall 1969), pp. 451–65.

The author is concerned with methodological and institutional problems faced by a social action agency in trying to make evaluation an important input to its policy process.

Wright, C. and H. Hyman. "The Evaluators," in Phillip E. Hammond (ed.), *Sociologists at Work.* New York: Basic Books, 1964, pp. 121–41.

This article reports on the evaluation of a summer institute for training young persons to be more effective democratic citizens. For the narration, the authors selected the literary device of a hypothetical interview about the project.

Yancy, Robert, Stewart Krawil, and John C. Rahiya. "The National Alliance of Businessmen: Its Purpose Interactions and Results," in Samuel Doctors (ed.), *Whatever Happened to Minority Economic Development.* Chicago: Dryden Press, 1974, pp. 74–80.

This is a good case study on the effectiveness of the NAB/JOBS program.

PUBLIC DOCUMENTS

Civil Rights: Progress Report–1970. Washington, D.C.: Congressional Quarterly, 1970.

Congress and the Nation: A Review of Government and Politics. Vol. II, 1965–68. Washington, D.C.: Congressional Quarterly Service, 1969.

"Design Report for the Opportunity Funding Corporation (OFC) Surety Bonding

Program," Contract No. BIC 5268, Boone–Young and Associates, August 1971.

Mangum, Garth L. "Evaluating Federal Manpower Programs," in *Employment and Training Legislation–1968,* prepared by the Subcommittee on Employment, Manpower and Poverty of the Committee on Labor and Public Welfare. Washington, D.C.: U.S. Senate, 1968.

Nathan, Richard R. *Jobs and Civil Rights.* Washington, D.C.: U.S. Commission on Civil Rights, April 1969.

National League of Cities. *Federal Budget and the Cities: A Review of the President's 1974 Budget in the Light of Urban Needs and National Priorities.* Washington, D.C.: National League of Cities, February 1973.

Nixon, Richard M. "Bridges to Human Dignity." Washington, D.C.: CBS Radio Network, April 25, 1968.

Office of Economic Opportunity. *Preliminary Results of the New Jersey Graduated Work Incentive Experiment.* February 18, 1970.

——. *Further Preliminary Results of the New Jersey Graduated Work Incentive Experiment.* May 1971.

——. *Standards for Evaluating the Effectiveness of Community Action Programs.* May 1969.

Opportunity Funding Corporation. *Case Studies and First Year Findings of OFC's Banking and Contractor Bonding Programs.* Washington, D.C.: Opportunity Funding Corporation, 1972.

——. *Measuring Financial Leverage of Indirect Financing Techniques.* Washington, D.C.: Opportunity Funding Corporation, 1972.

Public Papers of the President of the United States. Washington, D.C.: Office of the Federal Registrar, March 5, 1970.

"Statement by the President on Minority Enterprise," *Public Papers of the President of the U.S.* Washington, D.C.: Office of the Federal Registrar, National Archives and Records Service, March 5, 1970.

Stufflebeam, Daniel L. "Evaluation as Enlightenment for Decision-Making," paper presented to working conference on Assessment Theory, sponsored by Commission on Assessment of Education Outcomes, Evaluation Center, Ohio State University, 1968.

Suchman, Edward A. "Action for What? A Methodological Critique of Evaluation Studies," paper presented at the Annual Meeting of the American Sociological Association, 1968.

Trow, Martin. "Methodological Problems in the Evaluation of Innovation," paper presented to the Symposium on Problems in the Evaluation of Instruction, UCLA, 1967.

Weiss, Carol H. "The Politics of Evaluation," paper presented to the Annual Meeting of the Midwest Political Science Association, Chicago, March 1972.

——. "The Utilization of Evaluation Toward Comparative Study," paper presented to the Annual Meeting of the American Sociological Association, September, 1966.

The President's Advisory Council on Minority Business Enterprise. *Minority*

    Enterprise and Expanded Ownership: Blueprint for the 70's.
        Washington, D.C.: U.S. Government Printing Office, June 1971.

U.S. Congress, Joint Economic Committee. *The Analysis and Evaluation of*
        Public Expenditures: The PPB System. Washington, D.C.: U.S.
        Government Printing Office, 1969.

U.S. Department of Commerce. *Current Population Educational Attainment,*
        March 1972. Washington, D.C.: U.S. Government Printing Office,
        1973.

———. *Progress of the Minority Business Enterprise Program.* Washington, D.C.:
        U.S. Government Printing Office, January 1972.

———. Bureau of the Census. *Minority-Owned Businesses: 1969.* Washington,
        D.C.: U.S. Government Printing Office, August 1971.

———. Current Population Reports. *The Social and Economic Status of the Black*
        Population in the United States. Washington, D.C.: U.S. Government
        Printing Office, July 1972.

———. Office of Minority Business Enterprise, *Federal Programs Assisting*
        Minority Enterprise. Washington, D.C.: U.S. Government Printing
        Office, Summer 1971.

———. OMBE, *Report to the President on Minority Business Enterprise.* Washing-
        ton, D.C.: OMBE, June 30, 1970.

———, OMBE *MESBIC's and Minority Enterprise.* Washington, D.C.: U.S. Govern-
        ment Printing Office, December 1970.

———, Bureau of the Census, *1972 Survey of Minority-Owned Business Enter-*
        prises - Black. Washington, D.C.: Bureau of the Census, November
        1974.

———, *Fiscal Year 1974 Minority Business Development.* Washington, D.C.:
        OMBE, December 1974.

U.S. Department of Health, Education and Welfare, Public Health Service.
        Evaluation of Mental Health. Washington, D.C.: U.S. Government
        Printing Office, 1955.

U.S. Senate Committee on Labor and Public Welfare. *Indian Education: A*
        National Tragedy – A National Challenge. Washington, D.C.: U.S.
        Government Printing Office, 1969.

U.S. Small Business Administration, Office of Planning, Research and Analysis.
        Minority-Owned Businesses. Washington, D.C.: Small Business
        Administration (unpublished report), June 1969.

UNPUBLISHED PAPERS

Banner, David K. and Samuel I. Doctors, "Creative Inducements to Private
        Investment in the Minority Community: The OFC Approach,"
        Evanston, Ill.: Northwestern University Working Paper No. 107,
        72, 1972.

Brower, Michael J., "The Criteria for Measuring the Success of a Community
        Development Corporation in the Ghetto," unpublished manuscript
        from the Center for Community Economic Development, Cambridge,
        Mass., March 1970.

Buchanan, Garth N., Bayla F. White and Joseph S. Wholey, "Political Considerations in the Design of Program Evaluation," paper presented at the
American Sociological Association, Convention, 1971.

Campbell, Donald T., "Methods for the Experimenting Society," unpublished
manuscript, Northwestern University, Evanston, Ill., July 1972.

Caro, Francis G., "Evaluation Research and Client Participation," paper presented to the 1971 meeting of the American Sociological Association, September 1971.

———, "Social Research, Client Participation, and Local Agencies Serving the
Poor," unpublished manuscript, October 1971.

Coleman, J.S., "Problems of Conceptualization and Measurement in Studying
Policy Impacts," a paper presented at the Conference on the Impact
of Public Policies, St. Thomas, Virgin Islands, December 1971.

Hampden-Turner, Charles, *The Philosophy of Science,* unpublished manuscript.
Cambridge: The Center for Community Economic Development,
1972.

Helwig, Peter, Peter Lawrence and Nicolas Retsinas, *Economic Development in
Urban Neighborhoods: A Study of Community Development
Corporation,* unpublished paper, Cambridge, Mass.: Center for
Community Economic Development, January 1971.

Root, H. Paul and Patricia L. Braden, *A Study of the Sources and Uses of
Information in the Development of Minority Enterprise.* Ann Arbor:
University of Michigan Bureau of Business Research Working Paper
No. 14, 1970.

Rossi, Peter, "Practice, Method and Theory in Evaluating Social Action Programs," in Daniel Moynihan (ed.), *On Understanding Poverty:
Perspectives from the Social Sciences.* New York: Basic Books,
1969.

Starr, Joyce, "Taking Research Out of Academics and Into the Street," unpublished manuscript, Northwestern University Department of Sociology, 1971.

INTERVIEWS

Bloom, Devra. Interview. Office of Economic Opportunity, Washington, D.C.,
February 4, 1972.

Brazzel, Mike. Interview. Office of Economic Opportunity, Washington, D.C.,
February 26, 1972.

Cheney, Dick. Interview. Cost of Living Council, Washington, D.C., May 25,
1972.

Cross, Theodore. Interview. Sheraton Hotels, New York City, February 2, 1972.

DeGilio, James. Interview. Office of Economic Opportunity, Wahington, D.C.,
February 4, 1972.

Faux, Geoffrey. Interview. Center for Community Economic Development,
Cambridge, Massachusetts, July 7, 1972.

Feldman, Marvin. Interview. Fashion Institute of New York, New York,
     February 2, 1972.
Gloster, Jack. Interview. Opportunity Funding Corporation, Washington, D.C.,
     May 26, 1972.
Goldman, Hank. Interview. Office of Economic Opportunity, Washington, D.C.,
     February 26, 1972.
Kosrovi, Carol. Interview. Office of Economic Opportunity, Washington, D.C.,
     May 26, 1972.
London, Paul. Interview. Sheraton Hotels, New York City, February 2, 1972.
Lowitz, Don. Interview. Lowitz, Vihon, Stone, Kipnis & Gertz, Chicago,
     Illinois, July 7, 1972.
Mabie, John. Interview. A.G. Becker and Company, Chicago, Illinois, July 7,
     1972.
Nelson, Steve. Interview. Opportunity Funding Corporation, Washington, D.C.,
     Several times during 1972, 1973 and 1974.
Partridge, Tony. Interview. Office of Economic Opportunity, Washington, D.C.,
     February 26, 1972.

Index

About the Authors

Assistant Professor David K. Banner is a faculty member of the School of Administration, University of New Brunswick, Fredericton, N.B., Canada. Professor Banner teaches undergraduate courses in the areas of management of human resources, organizational theory, business policy, business and society and the management of change. He holds the Bachelor of Science degree in mathematics from the University of Texas (1963), the Master of Business Administration from the University of Houston (1968) and the Master of Arts in Sociology and the Doctor of Philosophy degrees from Northwestern University (1972).

Professor Banner has published widely in both U.S. and Canadian journals with some 14 journal articles either authored or co-authored. He is a co-editor of Doctors, *et. al. Whatever Happened to Minority Economic Development?* (Chicago: Dryden Press, 1974). His research interests include the future of post-industrial institutions, the management of change, the relationship between work and leisure, and the politics of social evaluation.

Samuel I. Doctors is Professor of Business Administration, Graduate School of Business, University of Pittsburgh. He was a member of the United States Office of Education Task Force on Minority Business Education and Training and a consultant to the Opportunity Funding Corporation in Washington. Professor Doctors holds a bachelor of Science degree from the University of Miami with majors in Mathematics and Physics. He has done graduate work in mathematics and history and holds a Doctor of Jurisprudence degree from the Harvard Law School and a Doctor of Business Administration degree from the Harvard Business School.

He has been a consultant for the Urban Training Center for the Christian Mission, the Eli Lilly Endowment, Associate Director of the President's Advisory Council on Minority Business Enterprise (PACMBE) for National

Strategy and Goals, a consultant to the Office of Economic Opportunity and a consultant to various private firms in management education and fair employment practices. He was the principal author of the final report of PACMBE.

He has authored such books as *The Role of Federal Agencies in Technology Transfer* (MIT Press, 1969); *The Management of Technological Change* (The American Management Association, 1970); *The NASA Technology Transfer Program: An Evaluation of the Dissemination System* (Praeger, 1971); Minority Enterprise and the President's Council (Cambridge: Ballinger, 1973); and *Whatever Happened to Minority Economic Development* (Dryden, 1974). His articles have appeared in such journals as the *Minnesota Law Review*, the *MSU Business Review*, the *Journal of Law and Contemporary Problems*, the *Business and Society Review*, *Business Perspectives*, and similar journals.

Andrew C. Gordon is Associate Professor of Sociology, Urban Affairs, and Psychology at Northwestern University. He received his Ph.D. in Social Psychology from Columbia University in 1970.

He has been the director of a variety of projects concerned with social action and the delivery of social services by public and private agencies. His articles have appeared in such journals as *Journal of Personality and Social Psychology, Northwestern University Law Review*, and the *Journal of Personality*, and he has contributed articles in a number of books.